The CAT'S OUT OF THE BAG

The CAT'S OUT OF THE BAG

Truth and lies about cats

MAX CRYER

EXISLE
PUBLISHING

First published 2015

Exisle Publishing Limited,
P.O. Box 60-490, Titirangi, Auckland 0642, New Zealand.
'Moonrising', Narone Creek Road, Wollombi, NSW 2325, Australia.
www.exislepublishing.com

A catalogue record for this book is available from
the National Library of New Zealand.

ISBN 978 1 921966 54 5

10 9 8 7 6 5 4 3 2 1

Text design and production by IslandBridge
Illustrations from shutterstock.com
Cover design by Christabella Designs
Printed in Shenzhen, China by Ink Asia

Contents

Acknowledgements

The author thanks Steve Jennings, Geoffrey Pooch, Paul Barrett, Clif Crane, Graeme & Valerie Fisher and Ian Watt for their assistance in the preparation of this book.

Introduction

Although usually referred to as a 'domestic' animal, it is far from clear just how far a cat fulfils the adjective 'domestic'. Owners of cats cherish the warm, furry presence in their household, and the cat goes along with maintaining this illusion of 'family' — so long as the food supply continues and the water bowl is fresh. But Pulitzer Prize-winning journalist George Will opined that: *The phrase 'domestic cat' is an oxymoron.*

And it is often said that it takes a while for cats to train humans to provide for the cat's needs (shelter, food, drink and safety) but not to expect anything in return. Horses carry, dogs retrieve, sheep are shorn, and cows give milk and provide meat and hides, as do lambs and pigs. Those creatures are often described as domesticated, but curiously are not always perceived as 'part of the family'. And yet a cat is definitely perceived as part of the family — although sometimes described as 'providing nothing'. The cat will not train for guard duties, herd cows or sheep, help blind people, or anything else — even just bringing in the newspaper. Writer David Michie's cat character, in *The Dalai Lama's Cat*, points out: *Whoever heard of a Pavlov cat?*

Of all the creatures which function close to the human lives — goldfish, horses, goats, guinea pigs, donkeys — only the cat can be called free. As Mr Kipling pointed out in 1902: *The cat walks by itself.* And it walks by itself in many guises: there are over 100 recognised breeds and a great many 'informal' outcomes. But curiously, in spite of variations, all cats are of a similar size, shape, weight and habit. A visitor from an alien planet could instantly recognise any of the hundred breeds as being cousin to the others.

The same cannot be said about the cat's nearest domestic partner — the dog. Put a Chihuahua next to a St Bernard, or a spaniel next to an Irish wolf-hound, then tell the alien they are the same thing, and watch him become confused. It would seem impossible to be simultaneously varied and unique, and yet be the same basic animal.

Cats, no matter how distant their breeds, retain a similarity of height, weight and basic shape.

But George Will's remark about cats' domesticity being an oxymoron, and Kipling's (admittedly accurate) description of their always walking alone, cannot be taken as a complete assessment of a cat's value. While it is pedantically accurate to say that like the lilies of the field, *they toil not, neither do they spin*, it is not fair to describe a cat as 'providing nothing'. The cat provides company, keeps human curiosity alert, and with its version of companionship brings food for the spirit. It is often beautiful, but suffers no pretensions, is impervious to rank, reduces the self-important to being humble and the aggressive to being calm. A cat is choosy and cannot be persuaded; it is servant to nobody ... but in its own way it adds a presence to the household which welcomes it.

For the person living alone, nine lives added to one makes a perfect ten.

– attributed to Jo Kittinger

By some estimates, they are the most popular household pet in the civilised world.

Anyone who has a cat understands why.

1
Words

A cat is defined by the *Oxford English Dictionary* as:

An agile, partly nocturnal, quadrupedal carnivorous mammal, *felis catus*, with smooth fur and retractile claws, long domesticated as a pet.

But at other times it has been described as:

- a furry keyboard cover
- a living alarm clock
- an ego covered with fur
- a small animal frequently mistaken for a meatloaf
- a petite extortionist
- grace, beauty, mystery and curiosity, in a companionable bundle
- mammal — not large, but with an attitude problem.

In his *The Devil's Dictionary*, Ambrose Bierce offers an alternative definition:

A soft, indestructible automaton provided by nature to be kicked when things go wrong in the domestic circle.

Cat

The word 'cat' appears to have settled down in English after a collection of words from both the African and Asian continents contributed to its development.

The Nubian *kadis*, and Berber *kadisha* and *quttah* from North African Arabic may have been factors in the version found in Byzantine Greek: *katta*.

In Latin this became *cattus* and *catta*. The Latinate word progressed through ancient German as *kazza* (later *katze*), old Dutch and Frisian as *katte*, old Norse as *kottr*, to old French as *cat* (later *chat*) and into old English as *catt*.

Then eventually: *cat*.

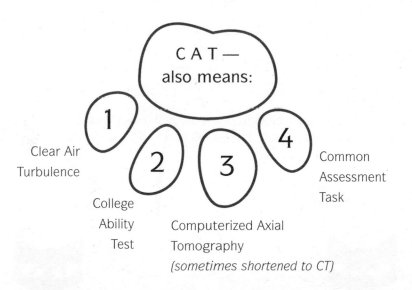

CAT—
also means:

1 Clear Air Turbulence

2 College Ability Test

3 Computerized Axial Tomography
(sometimes shortened to CT)

4 Common Assessment Task

'Cat'
in other languages

Armenian	katu	Icelandic	köttur
Basque	catua	Italian	gatto/gatta
Cherokee	wesa	Japanese	neko
Chinese	mao	Korean	ko-yang-i
Dutch	kattekop	Latin	cattus
Egyptian	kut	Maltese	qattus
Esperanto	kato	Maori	ngeru or poti
Estonian	kiisu	Polish	kot/kotka
Farsi	gorbe	Romanian	pisica
Finnish	kissa	Russian	koshka
French	chat	Saudi Arabian	biss
German	katze	Spanish	gato/gata
Greek (modern)	gata	Swahili	paka
Gujarat	bilaadi	Swedish	katt
Hebrew	chatul	Turkish	kedi
Hindi	billi	Ugandan	paka
Hungarian	macska	Zulu	ikati

Catfish

A fish family classified as *silurids* with many varieties, featuring sensory barbels around the mouth (resembling the whiskers of a cat) and a skin with no scales.

Copycat

A person who copies other people's actions, style, etc. The term may have been in use earlier, but its first known showing in print is in Constance Cary Harrison's *Bar Harbor Days* (1887):

> Our boys say you are a copy cat, if you write in anything that's been already printed.

The only known explanation is that it refers to the way kittens learn from their mothers by being shown an action, then copying it. Among cats, this may be regarded as a good thing — among human artists, designers, musicians, writers and other creators, it is not.

Catsilver

A name given to minerals which separate into thin leaves; also called *mica*, *isinglass* and *glimmer*.

Cat's-tail

A marsh-growing plant with long, flat leaves, which are used for weaving chair seats and baskets.

Catsfoot

A type of ground ivy, also known as Haymaids, Creeping Charlie, Hedgemaids and Alehoof. In centuries past it was used to flavour ale, and is still believed to have healing qualities, especially for tinnitus, chronic coughs, and indigestion. The plant is poisonous if too much is ingested. (Also known as *catspaw* and *alpine pussytoes*.)

Tabby

This word dates back to medieval Iraq, where a lustrous silk fabric with characteristic wavy stripes was manufactured in the district of Baghdad called Attabiyya. An abbreviated form of that name — *attabi* — became the description of the fabric itself. Eventually the fabric and the name began to be known in Europe, and the Anglicised form 'tabby' drifted into the English language during the seventeenth century. Initially it referred only to the luxurious stripey fabric. But by the end of that century the fabric's similar appearance to the pattern of certain cats with a striped and mottled coat gradually caused the name of the fabric to transfer to the cats in England. During the eighteenth century a 'tabby' could also mean an ill-natured, spiteful woman, then a complete turnaround in the 1900s saw 'tabby' refer to an attractive young woman. But these uses all faded — the fabric, the pretty young thing and the elderly gossip — and the name 'tabby' to describe certain cats has taken total ownership of the word.

Kitty

Although 'kitty' and 'cat' both refer to the same animal, the two words are not related to each other. The ancient Latin *cattus* travelled eventually into English as 'cat'. But in old Anglo-Norman French a young cat was known as a *chitoun*, which gravitated into Middle English as *kitoun* ... and that became 'kitten', or its abbreviation 'kitty'.

The same word when applied to money accumulating during a card game has different ancestry (see **The kitty**), and also when used in bowling (see **Bowls ... the kitty**).

Clowder and Kindle

Clowder is the correct term for a group of cats gathered together. It is not a word you hear very often — because it's a fairly rare occurrence to see a crowd of cats. You can see a herd of cows or a flock of sheep any day of the week, but cats don't normally gather in large groups; a lot of cats together is not a common sight. Hence we don't often need to use the word!

'Clowder' developed from two ancient words, *clot* and

clod, which were more or less interchangeable, both meaning a shapeless lump. Descendants of the two words are still around: 'clot' became applied to a shapeless lump in liquid (e.g. in milk or blood), 'clod' referred to a shapeless lump of something solid (e.g. soil).

But *clod* was also sometimes said as *clodder*, and it gradually developed an extra connotation: it was used to describe a shapeless disorganised mass or group which was accompanied by pandemonium and even noise.

By the late nineteenth century four descendants of the original words had settled into contemporary English:

- *clot* — a shapeless lump, but usually associated with liquid

- *clod* — another shapeless lump, usually solid

- *clutter* — a disorganised collection of objects, which in general remained still

- *clowder* — an untidy assembly of objects that did not remain still but moved around and possibly even made noise.

So although *clowder* is connected to *clutter*, over the centuries *clutter* has come to mean a messy collection of stationary things (think of a table after a four-course meal, or a teenager's bedroom), and *clowder* describes a group of objects or living creatures moving around independently of one another. Thus, *clowder* is the perfect word to describe an assembly of cats.

A very old use of the verb *to kindle* meant 'to give birth', usually applied to small creatures. Hence the expression: a *kindle* of kittens.

Catkins

The name is given to the flowering stem on some varieties of willow and poplar, where many fluffy non-petalled blooms feature on the sides of a long central axis ... slightly resembling the tail of a cat. The word comes into English from the Dutch word *katteken* – meaning 'little cat'.

Cathouse

This slang term for a brothel is derived from the archaic (fifteenth-century) use of the word 'cats' as a derisive term for prostitutes ... derived from the observation that when a female cat is in heat, male cats feel compelled to gather around her.

Tomcat

The term refers to any male cat, but also can refer to a man who enjoys the favours of many women.

Until the eighteenth century, male cats were often referred to as 'ram cats'. But a book by Henry Fielding written in England in 1760 was called *The Life and Adventures of a Cat*, and the 'hero' of the book was a male cat with a very active sex life. He was named Tom — and the name (and the image) has stuck ever since.

Sex kitten

The term 'sex symbol' has been in use since approximately 1910. But in 1956 when 22-year-old French actress Brigitte Bardot burst onto the screen in *And God Created Woman*, a variation in the expression arose — 'sex kitten'.

Worldwide, real kittens refrained from comment.

Caterwauling

The word has been in use in English since the fifteenth century, and has the (easily understood) meaning of making harsh and strident drawn-out sounds, often of a quarrelling nature. The reason that the meaning is so obvious is that the word is basically 'echoic' — the sound tells you what the word means, without further consultation.

It derives from *cat* — with the addition of an imitative 'yowl'. There is a similarity to an old German word, *katerwaulen*, which has the same structure and the same meaning. Either way, they are both 'imitative'.

Shakespeare was onto it in *Twelfth Night* when Sir Toby and Sir Andrew attempt to sing, and Maria exclaims: '*What a caterwauling do you keep here!*'

Mark Twain wrote a short book called *A Cat-tale* in 1880, to entertain his two young daughters and, in doing so, help them learn difficult new words, especially words which sounded as though they referred to cats — which they didn't. Words he chose included:

catacaustle	a caustic curve formed by reflection
catachersis	the mistaken wrong use of one word in place of another intended
catadrome	a word sometimes used to refer to a racecourse
catadupe	a dead and heavy sound
cataclysm	a violent upheaval
catamount	a type of tiger, the North American cougar
catapetalous	having petals which are held together by stamens
cataract	a great fall of water
catarrh	a discharge of mucous fluid into the bronchial passages
catechism	instruction by questions and answers
catemate	to connect in a series of links or ties

Webster's Dictionary (1879)

Sourpuss

Someone who is cranky. Some scholars assign the word's ancestry to an ancient word *buss* which referred to the 'face'. Over time, the word may have undergone a change in pronunciation (see **Puss**).

Catty remarks

Catty remarks are unkind comments, often (but not always) made by a woman, and often (but not always) about another woman. A vague association between women and cats has been around for centuries, and gained wider currency in the sixteenth century when John Heywood collected the saying '*A woman hath nine lives like a cat.*' Soon, a woman who gossiped about other women was said to be making 'catty' remarks about them.

Caddy

The Malayan word *katti* signifies a kind of weight, and it was the measure by which tea was usually packed, sold and transported. The Malayan word drifted into English and gradually became applied to the container holding the tea, rather than to its weight. And the anglicised version 'catty' eventually gave way to … 'caddy'.

Catgut

When cats decide to sing (especially male cats), the most devoted humans would find it difficult to describe the sounds as lovely music. The same applies to their being in distress. And there have been times in European history when the sounds of cats being tortured, even burned, were not uncommon. Their noises are believed to be the reason why the strings of musical instruments are identified as coming from inside cats, when in fact they do not.

As early as the 1600s there was comment about the sound of awkward and inept fiddlers scraping the 'guts of cats' — and based on the similarity of sound, the assumption had some credibility. But it isn't true. For centuries, musical instruments were customarily fitted with 'strings' made from sheep intestines — suitable cleaned, treated with certain marinades, dried, stretched and twisted. The result of all this is an impressive cord with great tensile strength and (in the right hands) capable of producing beautiful sounds.

Shakespeare gets it right in *Much Ado About Nothing*, when Benedict comments on Balthazar's lute playing: '*Is it not strange that sheep's guts should hale souls out of men's bodies?*'

Besides making music, the strong sheep-gut 'string' was widely used by archers as bowstrings, as well as for hanging the weights of long-case clocks, stitching surgical incisions, and for tennis racquets.

There were two other contributing factors to naming music strings as 'cat-gut'. Across Europe in medieval times, powerful superstitions were associated with the killing of cats. During that period, professional string-makers (who used sheep) deliberately put about the story that their 'strings' came from cats: a ploy to protect their livelihood, since anybody wanting to set up a rival string business would believe they had to face the killing of cats, and its ominous consequences.

There was also a very old word *kit*, meaning a small fiddle ... and referring to the fiddle's string as *kitgut*, meaning 'violin strings', may have brought about the misinterpretation in English of cat intestines being associated with violins. But that wasn't true.

In time, the invention of nylon and finely wound steel meant that many traditional stringings with sheep-made cords became a thing of the past. There is, however, a move back towards the 'warmer' sound that vibrating natural fibre makes.

Moggy

The word is usually used affectionately about a cat, but originally it carried a vague feeling that the cat being referred to was of fairly obscure background. Perhaps companionable, but not very sleek and glamorous.

'Moggy' has carried that sort of shadow around it for many years. The word is a variation on 'Maggie', which for many years was a rather derisive English term for a dishevelled old woman. The term 'a maggie' gradually shifted from old crones to cows (presumably because of their similarly inelegant bearing). 'Maggie' slowly changed into 'moggy', still meaning a lumbering cow or a shabby old woman.

But early in the 1900s, when the streets of London abounded with deprived alley cats, the word 'moggy' began to be used to describe these unfortunate creatures. Eventually the word moved onto cats in general — and it really stuck. 'Moggy' is now widely used to describe not just alley cats, but sometimes also their most elegant cousins.

Cattery

A place where cats are looked after. The word somehow gives the impression of being contemporary — but it has been in use since the late 1700s.

Catwalk

Obviously there is a connection between a cat's ability to walk along a narrow strip with no side support, and models sashaying along a raised ramp with no rail. But the word 'catwalk' isn't new; it has been in use since at least the middle of the nineteenth century or possibly earlier, when parts of sailing ships were known as *catwalks* and building sites used the same term for high, narrow communication bridges.

In approximately 1910 the term started to move into more common use, especially in connection with dirigible aircraft. A horizontal ladder-type structure inside the aircraft, on which the crew could move from one part to another, was called a *cat-walk*. Later, the term moved to other aircraft, and was used in World War 2 to describe the long plank which stretched between the cockpit and the tail inside bomber aircraft.

All these applications were sometimes called *cat's walk* rather than *catwalk* — but the 's' was gone by the time the term started being used in theatre and fashion shows, in approximately 1950. Prior to that, and even afterwards, the terms 'ramp' and 'walkway' were still being used to describe the long, narrow platform on which fashion models walked. But by the 1970s the word *catwalk* seemed to have become the universally used term.

Pussyfoot

A hunting cat can move gently and silently, on padded feet. Used metaphorically, pussy-footing means to behave in an overly cautious manner, timidly, and refraining from saying or doing anything definite. The term seems to have arisen in America late in the 1800s. Its wider popularity sprang from its being used by President Theodore Roosevelt in 1903.

Catcalls

When Samuel Pepys wrote in his 1659 diary that he had bought a *catcall*, he was referring to a whistle used at public performances to express disapproval. Theatre patrons who didn't have such a whistle imitated the sound of it by making 'wauling' noises like the cries of a cat. In the theatre, making catcalls can still express scorn.

Caterpillar

In old French, the caterpillar was known as *chatepelose* — 'hairy cat'. A version of the old French word may have transferred to English, where the original of 'caterpillar' was *catyrpel*, first seen in print in 1440. But two other English words influenced the final form. *Cater* has the sense of 'providing food', and the old form of *pill* was used to mean 'plunder' (surviving in the modern word 'pillage') — and caterpillars in full feast can certainly plunder the local greenery.

By 1775 when Dr Johnson published his famous dictionary, the spelling had settled into *caterpillar*. In the meantime, the French had modified their ancient word for caterpillar, *chatepelose*, into the more modern word *chenille* — a curious switch in imagery, considering *chatepelose* means 'hairy cat' and *chenille* is derived from the Latin for 'little dog'!

The kitty

The kitty is the pool of money paid in by participants in a common activity, the whole being used as winnings. There are two schools of thought about why it is called 'the kitty'.

One version links the expression to the old French card game of faro. The patron image of faro was a tiger — possible because images of a tiger were frequently associated with Chinese gambling houses. Reputedly a picture of a tiger was also hung outside venues where faro was being played. Gradually the accumulated betting money took on the name of the 'tiger' image … and over a period of time the 'tiger' was jocularly referred to as the 'kitty'. Not only did the name stick, but the use of it spread to a range of card games beyond faro, and to other activities involving participant-contributed money. Adding to this money was to *sweeten* (or *fatten*) *the kitty*.

However, diligent language students trace a connection between the 'kitty' in its sense of 'an accumulating pile of money' and an old British dialect word *kidcot*, which actually meant 'a place where young goats were kept', but which came to be a slang term for a prison. *Kidcot* developed into *kitcot*

and eventually *kitty* — and was attached to the money pool in card games, because the word had somehow developed a shade of meaning implying isolation and protection. Hence, the desired pool of money which could not be 'released' until someone won.

Bowls ... the kitty

In the game of lawn bowls, one white ball is stationary, and players roll their own bowling balls as close as possible to it, if possible knocking any opponents' bowls out of the way. We don't know whether Sir Francis Drake called that ball a 'kitty' when he was famously playing bowls in 1588, but that's the name widely used nowadays.

The reason for naming that ball *kitty* has been lost in the mists of time. One possibility has emerged: that the white ball, which is also known as the 'jack', developed a more feminine name when women took part in bowls. Hence, the *jack* for men, and the *kitty* for women. But if that story is true, the line has become very blurred. (The ball is also known as the *sweetie*, the *bill* ... and also sometimes — the *cat*!)

Hip cats

During the era of slave trading, many black slaves shipped to America took the African language of Wolof with them. Later generations of black Americans referring to a man as a 'cat' are believed to be using a derivative of the Wolof word *kai*, meaning a 'person'. During the early and mid-twentieth century, another Wolof word rose to prominence: *hipi*. In its home country, *hipi* means 'to be awake and aware — to be alive to what's going on'. Hence, we got people who were *hip* or *hep*, some of whom became *hepcats* — and others became *hippies*.

Polecat

Polecat is a complete misnomer, because the animal has nothing to do with cats. Its name arose from the Continental version of the creature being called in French a *poule chat* — a cat which stole hens. Because this took place only at night, there was confusion about what animal was actually doing the deed, and cats were blamed. The English version of the name was used to describe British ferrets (which are slightly different from their Continental cousins), and it stuck.

Although the polecat/ferret is often considered to be a mammal which is less-than-loveable, there have been periods in fashion when its fur was very desirable indeed. The ferret's fur was known as 'fitch', and is a close cousin to mink and ermine.

Catsuit

The *catsuit*, a form-fitting garment covering the whole body all in one piece, is thought to have derived its name from the costume customarily worn by a pantomime 'cat' — usually a slim dancer in a sleek form-fitting disguise.

The garment leapt to prominence in 1965 when Diana Rigg made a memorable impact on television viewers in *The Avengers*. Her character, Mrs Emma Peel, was not playing a cat, but in Britain the image of the young Ms Rigg became allied with her shapely high-fashion form-fitting catsuits.

Not long after, American television viewers were introduced to a similarly-clad Catwoman, played by Julie Newmar in *Batman* — and the catsuit was here to stay.

Cat's paw (knot)

Used for hooking tackle to the end of a rope, or attaching a rope to some object such as the branch of a tree. The knot consists of several characteristic twists which combine to make it especially secure.

Catshark

The catshark belongs to the large shark family Scyliorhinidae, which has over 150 species. They are believed to be known colloquially as 'catsharks' because of their elongated eyes, vaguely resembling those of a cat. Curiously, some members of the Scyliorhinidae family are also known colloquially as 'dogfish'.

Catnap

A fairly obvious derivation — cats' ability to sleep is legendary — but the *catnap* is characterised by two factors: it is brief (rather than settling in for a long, luxurious sleep) and it is 'dozing lightly' (rather than sleeping deeply). Like a cat, a person catnapping can come back to life fairly promptly. It is believed that the faculty of hearing is still active in a catnapping cat.

Catnip

The plant *Nepeta cataria* is a relative of ordinary mint, and, like mint, is pleasantly aromatic. But this version has an oil called *nepetalactone* whose particular aromatic quality might not enhance the flavour of green peas, but certainly gives cats a few minutes of pleasure. They will first sniff at the plant then tackle it with teeth, tongue, and rubbing their fur against it. Result: moderate but uninhibited ecstasy — after which normal behaviour is quickly resumed, as if nothing has ever happened. (Valerian has a similar effect.) Especially devoted cat-owners can buy 'essence of catnip' in aerosol form, for making a cat's toys or scratch-post more exciting.

Cat nip — the real thing

A protesting — or friendly — nip from a cat can easily be dismissed, but may also be more serious than it seems. In February 2014, America's *Journal of Hand Surgery* published a report from the Mayo Clinic on the danger of cat bites. Microsurgeon Dr Brian T. Carlsen explained that a dog with just as many germs in its mouth as a cat has blunter teeth, and leaves a bite wound that is easier to deal with. But cats' teeth are sharp and can penetrate very deeply, so they can transmit bacteria into the tissues and joints — good ways to breed infection. Even a small nip can cause a problem, and can introduce bacteria difficult to combat with antibiotics.

Dr Carlsen said that, because cat bites often look like a pinprick and dog bites look much worse, people tend to be more dismissive of cat bites than dog bites. But this is not wise. Over a survey period, the Mayo Clinic treated an average of 64 patients a year with cat-bite infections; of them, one in three required hospitalisation. Their advice: even a friendly nip can become inflamed, and if so must be medically treated immediately.

Ailurophile

A person who loves cats. The word arises from a Greek name for a cat goddess, *Ailuros*, strictly meaning 'the waving one' and based on the appearance of a cat's tail. A somewhat informal combining of *ailuros* with the Greek *phile* (loving) gives the English *ailurophile*.

Ailurophobe

The opposite: a person who dislikes cats or is even frightened of them. From the Greek *ailuros* (cat) plus *phobe* (fear).

Grimalkin

In the thirteenth century a woman of 'low class' was referred to as a *malkin*, sometimes thought to have originated as a diminutive for Matilda. In time *malkin* became restricted to old women — and then the word moved on to cats. Probably echoing the less-than-fashionable appearance of elderly women, the prefix *gri-* became attached (meaning 'grey'). Thus emerged *grimalkin*: a grey cat, or eventually any cat at all.

The pet cat of French astrologer and prophet Nostradamus was Grimalkin, and one of Macbeth's witches also has a pet of that name. Novelist Tracey Fobes was inspired to visualise the *grimalkin* as a legendary beast of ancient Scotland.

Gib

Neutered males among the beasts of the field — horses, bulls, sheep — are known by a name (gelding, steer, wether, respectively), and *gib* is a term which can be used for a neutered cat. Not often heard nowadays, *gib* was originally a term for any male cat, originating in a long-ago custom of calling male cats 'Gilbert'. This could have arisen in approximately 1400, when the major French classic *The Romance of the Rose* was translated into English, and the French name Tybalt came out as 'Gilbert — the cat'. But over the following two centuries a shift of emphasis took place, and *gib* became a reference to a neutered male cat — as referred to by Shakespeare in *Henry IV*: '*I am as melancholy as a gib cat.*'

A neutered (spayed) female cat is sometimes (rarely) referred as a *spey* or a *spay*.

Pussycat

Besides the obvious, the term is also used to describe a person who is likeable and gentle, sometimes unexpectedly so — such as a behemoth in the business arena or on the sports-field who is 'a pussycat at home'.

Grooming

A cat grooming itself is *autogrooming*. If it is grooming a friend, that is *allogrooming*.

Catseyes

Catseyes, the reflective buttons set in roads as a guide to drivers, were invented by British road-mender Percy Shaw, reportedly because one foggy night he was saved from driving off a twisting road by seeing his car's headlights reflected in the eyes of a nearby cat. His invention was patented in 1934. Britain soon had several million of them in position.

Catseye is also the name given to the semi-precious gemstone *chrysoberyl*, which when cut in a smooth, rounded shape reflects a thin, brightish streak of light — which resembles the contracted pupil of a cat's eye.

Puss

A conclave of scholars cannot agree on the exact derivation of the familiar word *puss*. Its origin may date back to several thousand years BC, from the Egyptian language's name for their cat goddess Bast (also translated as Pasht, Bastet or

Basht), which through the passage of centuries may have been modified in English as 'puss'.

But another theory points to a very old Lithuanian word sounding similar to 'puss', which seemed to apply to something furry: for instance, a kind of willow with furry knobbles. That word might have drifted into English to describe the furry willow, and also several other furry animals, and then eventually settled onto just cats.

Sometime, somewhere in Ireland, there was a word sounding similar to 'puss' which meant 'to make a pouting mouth' — and so Ireland is yet another possible place of origin.

Another theory designates *puss* as an imitative word, sounding something similar to the sound which a cat makes itself. Or could it have been an ancient word, *buss*, meaning 'mouth, lips, face' — which somehow mysteriously moved on to refer to a whole cat?

And there was also a word in ancient English — *pusa* — meaning a bag, with the connotation of being something soft and flexible ... which could have been applied to a soft and flexible cat.

They are all theories.

We are in Miss Marple territory: she would have said 'Nobody knows'. But the cats don't care.

Cats at sea

In spite of their well-known caution regarding actual contact with water, there has long been an association between cats and boats. Many nautical terms, often originating with sailing ships, involve the cat and are commonly used by seafaring folk. Some samples …

Cat-o'-nine-tails

A whip. In olden days, seamen were viciously flogged with a nasty device made up of nine separate knotted 'tails' attached to a whip handle, each tail with three knots. The weals left on the flesh resembled an attack from a large and vicious cat. The punishment pre-dates the name by many years, but the name has been in use since at least 1695, when it is mentioned in Congreve's play *Love for Love*.

Cat's-paw

is a common description for ripples on water, caused by a light breeze gently sweeping across surface water and causing transitory ruffling.

Cat-heads

Short horizontal beams projecting from each side of the bow, over which the anchor is hoisted clear of the water and secured. The association of the structure's name with 'cat' may or may not derive from a Danish word for a big pulley (*katblok*) or may be from the Latin for 'chain' (*catena*). Either way, the cat-head beam often had the face of a cat carved on it.

Because of their position, the *cat-heads* were also the source of another nautical tradition: they were customarily used as a lavatory. Suspended as it is directly over water, the cat-head provides support for direct discharge, and has a convenient natural wave-flushing system. So arose the (abbreviated) expression 'going to the *heads*'.

The ideal motive force for sailing ships was a wind from behind: hence products dispersed at the front of the ship were blown away from the rest of the ship, whereas any 'discharge' from the stern would blow *forward* over everyone.

Long after sailing ships were a thing of the past, seamen referring to a toilet retained the description *the heads*, and the expression is sometimes heard beyond the sea. (But the original is plural: referring to the *head* apparently identifies the speaker as a landlubber.)

Cat tackle

The strong rope or cable which draws the anchor from the water and towards the cat-head, to secure it (sometimes called the 'handy billy').

Cat the anchor

When the anchor has been drawn up from the water ('weighed'), it needs to be kept clear of the ship. *Catting* the anchor is to hitch it into a horizontal position and secure it against the hull of the ship.

Whiskers

These are long spars which project from either side of the bow. They hold the *whisker stays*, which are rope or cable, reaching forward to support the bowsprit.

Catboat

Some seagoing terms vary in meaning from place to place. *Catboat* is a strange one, because it has two distinct meanings — more or less the opposite of each other. One use has *catboat* as a strong vessel for carrying up to 600 tons of coal or timber. But in contemporary times the term *catboat* is more often applied to a small, single-masted leisure craft. The context in which the word appears usually makes clear which of the two meanings is intended.

2
Around the world

Havana Brown

The cats known as Havana Brown are bred from black cats with Siamese cats. There are two schools of thought about where their name came from: either by comparing their rich deep-brown fur with the colour of a Havana cigar, or with the similar colour of the brown Havana rabbit.

The Savoy

One night in 1898 at the acclaimed Savoy Hotel in London, millionaire diamond merchant Woolf Joel held a dinner totalling 14 people ... but at the last minute, one guest had to drop out, leaving just 13 at table. Another guest somewhat pessimistically predicted that this might mean that one of the 13 would soon die. A few weeks after that dinner — millionaire Woolf was shot dead.

Naturally the hotel was mortified, and took an unusual step to overcome the problem of 13 on any future occasion: a member of staff was to sit at the table to make up the numbers. Later, in 1927, they went a step further, when architect/designer Basil Ionides was commissioned to sculpt a wooden cat, nearly a metre high and pure black. The cat became Kaspar, and was permanently available from then on to sit at any table where 13 people found themselves at a Savoy dinner when 14 had been intended.

Vietnamese zodiac

The Vietnamese zodiac system includes the cat — in the same position that zodiacs elsewhere usually feature a rabbit. But historically, Vietnamese are believed to have little regard for rabbits, whereas cats are more useful in capturing rats raiding valuable crops.

The Vietnamese person born under the sign of the cat is seen to be: positive; ambitious; creative; conservative; talented; and to have good judgement. But is also inclined to be: superficial; self-indulgent; stubborn; and to be subject to mood swings.

According to the Vietnamese zodiac, you know you are of the cat sign if you:

- feel comfortable in social situations, but also when being alone
- never want to settle down or be committed to one person or one thing
- listen to yourself and don't care what others think.

You are less compatible with people born under the rat, the rooster or the dog.

Some famous people born into the Year of the Cat: Nicholas Cage, Brad Pitt, Quentin Tarantino, Johnny Depp, Andy Warhol, Francis Ford Coppola.

Argentina

Cats up a tree aren't uncommon. But usually they come down, either on their own or with help. (Their claws are shaped for effective traction upwards, but are not so efficient for the reverse trip.)

News from Argentina in the late 1940s told of a cat named Mincha in Buenos Aires, who had climbed up a tree 40 feet high (12 metres) and showed no inclination to come down. In fact she stayed there for six years. The locals pushed up food and containers of milk on long poles, and Mincha seemed content to remain in her high-rise. Reports tell discreetly that she couldn't have been 'lonely for companionship', since she gave birth to three litters of kittens while living in the tree tops.

Amsterdam

De Poezenboot is a cat shelter floating in a canal in central Amsterdam. In 1966 Henriette van Weelde took pity on the growing number of stray cats around her Amsterdam house and began taking them in. Things began to get out of control when she became known as 'the cat lady' and people started bringing cats to her. Eventually in 1968 she bought an old Dutch sailing barge, and converted it into a houseboat of feline-friendly accommodation. Strays, discarded animals and sick ones gradually filled the space, and caring folk came on board to help look after them.

Within three years a second, bigger boat was needed, this time especially fitted out to be cat-friendly. Besides cats and helpers came sight-seers … and the two cat-sanctuaries floating on the Singel canal became a kind of tourist attraction! In 1979 the earlier boats were replaced by a custom-built ark.

In 1987 the sanctuaries were registered as an official charity — *Stichting de Poezenboot*, the 'Cat Boat Foundation'.

Cat's claw

Cat's claw is a vine in the Amazon area, which grows wrapped around jungle trees. It has been used for hundreds of years as a medicine for arthritis, gastritis and other illnesses.

Switzerland

In Switzerland, a particular Animal Protection Ordinance acknowledges that animals of 'socially living species' need adequate contact with their own kind. Cats able to leave the house and roam do not need a live-in companion, as they can choose to socialise with other cats. But if a cat cannot leave the house (such as when living in a high-rise apartment) then *it must be provided with a second cat as a 'social contact' or 'playmate'*. In September 2008 this Ordinance passed into Switzerland's national law and became a legal necessity.

Feline resorts

Not every nation offers them, but Britain and the United States have a wide variety of 'feline resorts' where cats can board when their owners are on holiday. They have names like: Cat Chalets; Club Pet; Cat Hotel; Paradise Pet Spa; Cat Nap Inn; or Feline Bed & Breakfast.

Amenities vary, but at the high-spend end, comforts offered to puss include: climate-controlled suites; multi-storey solo-tenant 'condominiums'; relaxing background music; cat furniture; jingle mice; laser-beam play-lights; daily room service; videos or selected TV programmes; ear cleaning; pedicures; privacy curtains; and massage therapy.

Secret life

A BBC television documentary *The Secret Life of the Cat* monitored 50 cats for 24 hours a day, in a small English village. Dr John Bradshaw (Bristol University) and Dr Sarah Bradshaw (Lincoln University) revealed life beyond the cat-flap with cat-cameras and electronic devices to record the cats' wanderings. The controlled electronic study demonstrated that domestic cats with access to surrounding ground territory can roam nocturnally from 50 metres to as far as 3200 metres (two miles) away from their home. Analysis of the various signallings (with scent and spray) showed how cats will establish, defend and even expand 'their' territory.

Bereavement

In Britain and the United States, Pet Bereavement Hotlines offer phone lines for 'animal-loss listening'. They provide counselling for grieving and for 'the devastation of suffering loss from the death of a pet'. While cats and dogs are the most frequent focus of feelings of loss, some services also include 'grief support' for the loss of birds and horses.

New Zealand

During the 1980s, an eccentric cat leapt to prominence in New Zealand. Named Rastus, he developed a taste for riding on his owner's motorbike — and frequently did so, always equipped with helmet and goggles. When an alert tea-packaging company featured the bike-travelling Rastus in television commercials, he rapidly became the subject of a popular song and 10 children's books. Rastus and his owner were both killed in a car crash in 1998, and a nation mourned.

Hotels

Ever keen to please customers, parts of the hotel industry have experimented with differing ways of letting the staff know not to intrude with mop and broom on a still-sleeping inhabitant. The traditional *Do Not Disturb* sign has been replaced in some places with elegantly designed images of *Dreaming*, or door-hangers featuring a brief but elegant verse referring to the beauties of sleep.

The door-hanger of one American hotel chain featured no words — just a sketch of a cat napping. Which led to the Riverbend luxury resort in Wisconsin going one step further: each room in the hotel is provided with a stuffed toy cat, stretched out in sleep. Placed outside the door at night, it is an instant message that the 'people indoors' are also asleep. If the toy cat appeals, it can be added to the bill and put into the luggage.

America issued official postage stamps featuring cats in 1988. They were not the first nation to do so. Cats and cat folklore have been featured on the official postage stamps of Germany, Panama, Hungary, Poland, Colombia, Monaco and Paraguay.

Harry Potter caused sufficient interest in Taiwan for an issue of stamps commemorating scenes from the movies. One, picturing the *Prisoner of Azkaban* scenario, included a suitably malevolent image of Crookshanks, the Hogwarts cat.

In the same vein, Dr Seuss's *Cat in the Hat* featured on a set of American stamps celebrating the birthday of Theodore Geisel ('Dr Seuss').

Los Angeles soprano Mary O'Brien had a favourite cat of eccentric temperament, called Dumbcluck.

A breed of cat in eastern Turkey, near the Van Lake, likes to swim. The Van cat's fur is not as thick as that of other cats, so when wetted it dries much more quickly. The cats frequently take a voluntary dunking in order to catch frogs in the lake. They are predominantly white, with ginger and brown markings around their head and tail, and their forehead carries a white patch known as 'The thumbprint of Allah'.

Sphynx cats have (quite naturally) no hair. They were developed in Canada in 1966, and, although hairless, are so warm to the touch that they are sometimes called 'hot-water-bottle cats'.

Cat racing

While the sport of racing horses, dogs and people is common enough, it is difficult to imagine arranging sport based on cats racing each other. But there are reports that it has happened.

In June 1860 Harrison Weir (founder of Britain's National Cat Club) wrote that in Belgium cat-racing had become a sport in high favour.

> In one of the suburbs of Liège it is an affair of annual observance during carnival time ... The cats are tied up in sacks, and as soon as the clock strikes the solemn hour of midnight the sacks are unfastened, the cats let loose, and the race begins. The winner is the cat which first reaches home, and the prize awarded to its owner is sometimes a ham, sometimes a silver spoon.

This hardly tallies with the image of what we usually perceive as 'racing'. (And one wonders how the winner was identified ... was every householder's report of the arrival time to be believed?)

In the 1930s news stories started to appear commenting on the opening of a more 'traditional' race-track for cats in England. The *Charleston Daily Mail* (31 July 1937) reproduced a story from the *Reader's Digest*:

> The first cat-racing track in the world was opened recently in the village of Portesham, England. The technique used is similar to that of greyhound racing,

but instead of a hare, the cats chase an electric mouse over a 220-yard course, each cat wearing a colored ribbon round its neck. The cats run at about half the speed of greyhounds, but are more intelligent and maneuver cleverly for position. Tabbies are considered the best racers. At present ordinary pets are used. If the sport grows, scientific breeding may produce faster cats for racing purposes only.

Later reports mentioned that the dwindling success of cat racing resulted in its fading out after 10 years.

But in 1987 *The Dorset Village Book*, written by Harry and Hugh Ashley, reported that the 'news' about the cat racing having taken place was all a hoax, and cats photographed being 'weighed in' were actually strays hastily gathered and dumped onto a pub's scales.

Which could explain why news of the Portesham cat racing was sparse — *and* that Rudyard Kipling was right again: a cat prefers to walk by itself.

Wing Commander 'Dambuster' Guy Gibson VC used to take his cat, Windy, with him on many flights, even seriously dangerous ones. The cat was believed to have gained more flying hours than many human pilots.

French writer Colette had two favourite cats: Muscat and Kapok.

The prophet Mohammed, founder of Islam, had a pet cat called Muezza. Legend has it that he loved his cat so much and respected its wish not to be disturbed that, once when Muezza went to sleep on the wide sleeve of his robe, when he needed to move away Mohammed gently cut the sleeve off and left it there, rather than disturb the cat.

The Isle of Man

If indeed Noah slammed the ark door on the tail of the last creature to board the ark — a cat from the Isle of Man — then we know why the breed has had no tail ever since.

Alas, a more pragmatic explanation has the Manx cat as a rather unfortunate breed with a genetically deformed backbone, which leaves it without a tail and also affects the shape of the legs — and causes the cat to be unable to mate with its own kind and produce non-deformed offspring. A tailless Manx cat must always be mated with a tailed one in order to ensure that the litter is not stillborn or misshapen.

There are many fanciful myths about the Manx losing its tail: this little poem brings Noah back into the story — but with a slightly different spin:

> Noah, sailing o'er the seas,
> Ran fast aground on Ararat.
> His dog then made a spring and took

The tail from off a pretty cat.
Puss through the window quick did fly,
And bravely through the waters swam,
Nor ever stopp'd 'til high and dry
She landed on the Isle of Man.

Anon

Although unrelated to the Manx breed, the 'Bobtail' cats of Japan also have no tail. But just to confuse the punter, the lack of tail in the Japanese variety, and the similar quality of the Manx, relate to two entirely different genetic aberrations, which just happen to produce the same result.

Queen Victoria — ever loyal to Scotland — had a favourite cat called White Heather.

Artistic expression

A somewhat mysterious organisation called The Museum of Non-Primate Art fosters knowledge about the 'artistic expression of non-primates species'. This (reputedly) includes moles who tunnel in patterns, horses who put forth dung into pyramids — and cats who dance and do painting. Thought to be located near Chichester, the museum is alas not available for public visiting, but enthusiastically fosters paintings done by cats, and photo-studies of cats dancing, on its website, to which contributions arrive from all over the world and are featured (www.monpa.com). If a cat shows inhibitions, or any resistance to dancing, MONPA has a special CD available to encourage moggies in doing some fancy stepping.

Japan

In 2003 the Japanese launched a device called a 'Meow-lingual' which claims to be able to translate and interpret what your cat is 'saying'. A small hand-held unit, it contains a microphone and an inbuilt computer system carrying hundreds of pre-recorded mewings, categorised into various emotions or situations — hungry, bored, jealous, cross, sad, happy, has a fur ball, or has left a dead mouse in the hallway. When the unit is held close to the cat in mid-meow, the computer identifies which category the meowing most resembles and shows the answer on its screen. Pragmatists declare the 'translator' to be more accurately an 'emotion analyser'.

But as a bonus, the screen can also advise you about cat astrology, and the moods of your cat's particular star sign.

Tennis champion Jimmy Connors had a cat called Kismet.

Cat museums

There are two notable cat museums. In Malaysia, a 1987 exhibition of cat artefacts in the Kuala Lumpur museum was taken to Kuching ('the Cat City') under the care of the Sarawak Museum, and is now established as a totally independent cat museum. Regarded as a 'Cat Information Centre', the museum is situated on a hill with magnificent views, and encourages meetings between cat enthusiasts and researchers.

In Russia, the Moscow Cat Museum has a vast collection connected with cats in life and in art, including paintings, graphics, batiks, tapestries, collages, costumes, calendars, postcards, albums, ceramics, sculptures, glassware, dolls and photography. This part of the exhibition includes more than 1500 items and is constantly expanding. Besides these, books, souvenirs, photographs, films, cartoons, toys and postcards abound, all connected with cats. There are songs about cats, cat film festivals, theatre and dancing groups, cat 'fashion shows', and an annual beauty contest 'Woman & Cat', where the jury evaluates the beauty and grace of the pair. Also at least once a year an exhibition is mounted of children's paintings of cats. The museum tours parts of its collection throughout Russia and occasionally to other countries.

The town of Kittyhawk in North Carolina became famous as the venue for the Wright Brothers sustained power flight in 1903. Less famous is the reason for the town's name, which is derived from a Native American (Algonkian) word *chickahauk* — the meaning of which, over the years, has been completely forgotten.

In Korea, a very tiger-like cat called Hodori has been familiar in folklore and legends for decades. In 1988 he became the symbol for the Seoul Olympic Games.

Pet-centric

Among hostelries which accept pets, the Cypress Inn in Carmel, California, is recognised as one of the most liberal. Established by movie star Doris Day — a renowned cat-lover — the inn enhanced its pet services so that cats, dogs and cage-birds are welcome, pet-sitters are available (cats and dogs may not be left unattended), foods are available for pets (but not for people), and a list is posted of those local restaurants which permit pets to accompany their owners at lunch and dinner.

Mountain climbers

The London *Times* of 7 September 1950 reported that a kitten followed a group of mountain climbers leaving the Hornli Ridge to head up the Matterhorn in Switzerland. To the surprise of the climbers, the kitten later joined them at the Solway hut at 12,556 feet (3827 metres). Surprise turned to astonishment when the kitten gamely battled on, right to the Swiss summit and then the Italian summit — a climb of 14,000 feet (4267 metres). At the mountain peak, a guide who was aware that cats climb downwards less easily than they climb upwards put the kitten into his rucksack and took it back to base.

President Theodore Roosevelt's pet cat, Slippers, was allowed to attend official dinners with him.

Angora cats are named after the Turkish city in which they were first found — which later had its name changed to Ankara.

Money cats

There is no strict rule about which type of cat can be called a *money cat*, but generally the term describes parti-coloured or 'piebald' cats, whose fur has any combination of three colours. In America 'money cat' is interchangeable with 'calico cat', meaning a cat with three colours (in some countries calico is a totally plain fabric, but early American calico was often multi-coloured).

The only known story behind the term *money cat* dates back to an ancient Dutch legend about a poor milkman whose clients collected their milk from his house and left payment of coins pushed under his door. Thieves learned to flick the coins out again, using a rose-bush stem. But the milkman's multi-coloured cat learned a trick too: when the coins appeared under the door, she pawed them out of reach and, should a rose stem appear probing around, she seized it and ripped it away from thieving hands. Hence the milkman received all the money due to him because of his 'money cat' — and then everyone in the village wanted one, too!

The Oriental money cat

The folklore of Japan tells that, during the seventeenth century, Gotoku-ji Temple just outside Tokyo was beset by poverty. But the Buddhist abbot loved his cat, and no matter how difficult their finances were, he maintained and fed his pet. One day he told the cat that a serious crisis now loomed: good luck was needed, some income was essential, or the temple would have to be disbanded. The cat went out to the road beside the temple and sat preening himself (the way cats do), as a storm began to brew. Soon afterwards, a passing samurai lord and his warriors stopped to shelter under a nearby tree. The samurai lord saw the cat's paw raised as if beckoning to him, so he and his men approached the cat. As the lord and his men moved away from the tree, it was struck by lightning. The cat had saved their lives. The warriors took shelter in the temple, and, to reward the abbot for his willingness to show them hospitality, the samurai warriors became benefactors of the temple, and restored it to wealth and honour — thanks to that 'lucky cat'.

Word spread, and people began placing figurines of beckoning cats in their homes, shops and temples, believing it would bring them good luck and prosperity. From then on, the cat with its paw upraised became a symbol for good luck and good fortune.

Gotoku-ji Temple now contains a statue of its original benefactor cat — and many other cat tributes as well. Visitors go there to pray that the cat will bring them the same luck and prosperity it brought to the monks of the past.

Models of the original cat — with paw upraised — are called 'Maneki Neko', and can often be seen in Japanese homes, shops, businesses and restaurants. Sometimes his upward paw is waving; a discreet internal battery helps to draw the good fortune towards himself and 'wave' it into the premises. The 'money cat' or 'good fortune cat' has also been adopted in other places in the Orient and in Oriental business-places throughout the world.

Maneki Neko cats can be made of porcelain, wood, metals, ivory or pottery, are usually red-and-gold or black-and-white, and besides being harbingers of fortune they often do double duty — as money boxes.

Preservation

The practice of mummification of the dead did not vanish after the end of the ancient Egyptian era. In contemporary times the Summum Modern Mummifications company in Genesee Avenue, Salt Lake City, Utah, offers that a departed loved one from one's family can have 'Eternal Memorialization through Mummification'. The process is 'permanent, enduring, and timeless' with 'qualities of beauty, care, love, integrity, and protection'.

Mummifying a beloved pet is also among the firm's services. For a cat, the process can take between four and eight months. The cost — depending on the size of the cat, and on the quality of mummification and of the 'mummyform' (the stylised cat-form container, usually made of bronze) required — can be between US$4000 and US$50,000.

Another possibility is cloning. Founded in 1998, Massachusetts-based company PerPETuate (plus other companies such as Genetic Savings and Lazaron) seeks to arrange for 'banking' some DNA of a pet, from which a clone can later be engendered *when cloning becomes technically and financially more feasible'*. For pet-lovers, a clone of a departed loved one will help 'mute the sense of loss' and PerPETuate announces that its

vision lies in the future, represented by the ultimate breeding technology and presenting distinctive breeding opportunities to produce extraordinary, matchless, one of a kind, physically superior, brilliant, and innately talented replacements for lost pets. Unlike careful breeding, where only half of the desired genetic traits can be transferred to the new kitty or puppy, cloning transfers all of your pet's genes to cloned kittens and pups!

Collection and 'banking' of DNA involves:

1. Tissue samples collected by a veterinarian.

2. The samples shipped overnight to the laboratory.

3. Cells containing DNA are grown from those tissues.

4. Those cells are then stored in Bio-Kennels.

So far, in various pet 'banks' there are stored DNA cells from cats, dogs, horses, a cow, a goat and a ferret.

Chinese calendar

In the Oriental lunar calendar still followed by the Chinese, a cycle of 12 years allocates each year into the guardianship of a different animal. The cat is notably absent. Legends abound as to why the cat was omitted from the list (originally made by Buddha). Some kind of altercation between the cat and the rat figures in most versions, or that the rat had once fetched medicine for Buddha when he was ill, but the cat — not knowing this — later caught the rat and ate it. But the legend which most cat-lovers prefer to believe is that when Buddha gathered all of the animals together in order to make his choice of 12, the cat was asleep and missed the meeting.

New York

The *Journal of the American Veterinary Medical Association* reported on data gathered about city cats being treated by New York City vets after falling from buildings. Analysis showed that there was a 90 per cent survival rate, and that cats falling from higher than a seventh floor had fewer injuries than those falling from lower levels.

The explanation given: that when cats fall, they have a reflex action which allows them to shift their bodies mid-air into a position which allows for minimum impact, landing on their feet, thus lessening possible fractures. The higher the fall, the more time is available for the mid-air positioning to be assumed. A short fall — say from lower than seven floors — doesn't allow time for the cat to assume the 'parachute' shape, and landing injuries can result.

(The report was treated with some caution by those who pointed out that it was based on visits to the vet by cats who had survived a fall. But how many didn't? Cats already dead didn't make it onto the vet-visit list, thus somewhat weakening the quoted statistic.)

In July 2011, the *New York Post* and CBS reported that 16-year-old cat Gloucester survived a plunge from the twentieth storey of a New York apartment. The family had gone away for a few days, and had inadvertently left one window open a very small gap. When their pre-arranged cat-sitter came to feed the pet — he wasn't there. After asking around the building, the cat-sitter was taken by a security guard to the ground floor, where a passer-by on the street had found the bewildered cat Gloucester, a bit groggy, but apparently unharmed.

A visit to the vet confirmed that nothing external or internal appeared to be damaged, although for a few days Gloucester was — quite understandably — a bit wobbly and cautious.

Mayoral candidate

The town of Talkeetna in Alaska is classified as an 'historical district', so the position of its mayor is purely symbolic, rather than authoritatively functional. In 1997 the citizens had only mild enthusiasm for potential candidates in the forthcoming mayoral election — and a joke arose about launching a cat named Stubbs as a candidate.

Originally found left in a parking lot, Stubbs had become a very familiar figure about the town. Named after his blunted tail, he gradually had become loved by all. Electoral votes poured in — and Stubbs won, paws down.

The general store became his 'mayoral chambers', mayoral duties being fulfilled by frequent roams around town, inspecting bars and the drinkers therein (himself drinking from a wineglass laced with catnip), and attracting up to 40 tourists a day, who want to 'meet the mayor'.

Seventeen years after his appointment, the citizens still find Stubbs to be a purrfect public figure.

3

Bodies and behaviour

Breeds

There are over 100 formally recognised breeds of cat, with identifiable characteristics of the breed they claim, and pedigrees traceable back through several generations. Besides those, any neighbourhood may have other 'non formally recognised' strains of moggy which are certainly cats, just not with traceable pedigrees. Although there is variation in appearance among the 100 formal breeds, there is comparatively little difference in the build, weight, size and general demeanour of all cats.

Humans have 206 bones; cats have 245 bones. The greater number gives them greater flexibility. A cat is one of the few animals that can lick the middle of its own back.

Forty per cent of cats are ambidextrous.

Some cats can jump five times their own height. How does a human stack up? Cuban jumper Javier Sotomayor, who is 1.95 metres tall (6 feet 5 inches), won Olympic gold with a jump of 2.45 metres (8 feet), which, admirable though it was, is less than one and a half times his own height.

Grooming

So fastidiously clean are cats that it has been estimated that during its life the average cat spends 30 per cent of the time grooming itself. And in doing so, it loses almost as much fluid as it loses in urine.

Unlike humans, cats appear to wash *after* they have had a meal. This may be because of an old legend that once when a sparrow was caught in a cat's claws, he chided the cat for planning to eat him without first washing its paws and face. Embarrassed, the cat prepared to wash by temporarily putting the sparrow down. But the sparrow, taking advantage of this 'temporary' respite, immediately took the opportunity to fly away. From then on, cats have always eaten first, washed later.

A cat's tongue has little spikes which point backwards ... to aid in the fastidious practice of fur-grooming.

Movement

A cat walks by stepping with both its left legs together then both right legs. And when they walk, their back feet land in the same places their forefeet just left. This is said to be a remainder of their original lives in the wild — making less 'foot' noise and fewer tracks, and providing more confident footing if the terrain turns rough.

In extremis — such as when they are in a hurry — their normal left-legs-stepping-together and right-legs-stepping-together quickly modifies into a faster 'diagonal' gait, with the opposite hindlegs and forelegs moving simultaneously.

A healthy cat with a strong impulse to be somewhere else can sprint at 30 miles per hour (48 kph).

The domestic cat is the only animal with a tail which, when walking along, it can hold directly upright (but only when it feels like it). No other species of cat does this: their tails are at right angles to the ground, thus horizontal, or hanging down and slightly tucked in.

Hearing

Human adults in good health can hear noise of 20,000 cycles per second. Dogs' ears can identify cycles up to 40,000 per second. Cats leave them all behind: their ears sort out sounds up to 100,000 per second, so a cat is able to hear tones two octaves higher than a human can, and even higher in pitch than a dog can. This is an aid to tracking small high-squeaking creatures such as mice.

(There is a school of thought that claims a cat will pay attention to you if you speak to it in the highest falsetto you can manage ...)

Many white cats with blue eyes are deaf.

There are approximately 30 muscles in a cat's ear; a human has six. Each ear can be rotated separately through 180 degrees — thus detecting and analysing noises from two directions simultaneously.

Eyesight

Cats easily see things at a distance, but sometimes not so well close-up (especially right underneath their nose). Hence — whiskers, which act as navigators and sensors of distances, detectors of air currents (revealing tiny movements nearby, such as those made by a mouse) and whether an opening is wide enough for the body to get through. The whiskers are twice as thick as hair, and are deeply rooted in highly sensitive nerve tissue. Since they are very much in touch with the nervous system, the whiskers can instantly convey a mass of information: measurement of space, air movement and pressure, collections of impressions which help estimate the movement and shape of potential prey. There are usually 24 whiskers, and they can be moved forwards, backwards and downwards, some groups independently of the others.

Other similar though less apparent whiskers are situated above each eye, and on the back of the front legs just above the paws.

Eminent veterinarian and prolific author on pet care Dr Bruce Fogle explains that the sensitivity of a cat's whiskers is such that they are 'capable of detecting anything that displaces them by a distance 2000 times less than the width of a human hair'.

Cats have peripheral vision of 285 degrees.

Scent

A cat has scent glands on its cheeks, forehead, tail, chin and rump, and under the toes. All of these can bestow a minute quantity of scent which no human can detect, but which is a page of information for another cat. Doing so is not necessarily being aggressive, simply the marking of a presence.

Rubbing itself against your leg, the cat isn't necessarily giving the equivalent of a hug or nuzzle. It is in fact seeking reassurance. The cat is checking that the slight scent it deposited on you before you left the house (from little glands in its face and the base of its tail) is still there when you get home.

The cat's tail can convey at least 10 separate signals, expressing what it wishes to communicate at the time — ranging from peaceful relaxation (tail in gentle downward curve, and perked up a bit at the tip), to active aggression against a perceived enemy (tail straight in the air and bristled).

A cat's sense of smell is infinitely more sensitive than a human's. According to the Faculty of Veterinary Science at Pretoria University, humans have about 5 million olfactory cells (to identify smells), while cats have approximately 100 million.

A cut onion rubbed on a no-go surface will deter cats, as they don't like the smell. They are not keen on vinegar either — the acidic fumes irritate a cat's respiratory system. And the crushed leaves of the aromatic herb rue give out an aroma which cats hate; rue has been recognised since AD1 as a repellent to cats.

Tiny bumps and ridges on a cat's nose form the equivalent of a human fingerprint, as every cat's nose 'print' is unique — just as every human's fingerprint is.

Don't look too shocked if Puss presents a litter in which several kittens have differing colours, and are even of different breeds. This is because cats are capable of *superfecundation*: fertilisation within the female's reproductive tract by sperm from more than one contributor. Thus, if mama has been in a generous mood, her available ova may well be fertilised by contributions from several enthusiastic partners ... thus producing differing kittens (who are in fact only half-siblings).

Taste

Cats have few taste receptors on the tongue which respond to sugar, and in general are not interested in sweet things — which is a help to their health, since their body has a low tolerance to sugar.

Cats can seem to enjoy a snack containing chocolate, but chocolate contains a dangerous ingredient which is toxic to cats.

Aspirin is poison to cats.

Besides their molars and incisors, cats have two teeth on the upper jaw fourth from the centre on each side, officially called the 'canine' teeth. Most cats are too embarrassed to mention this.

Cats don't chew; their very strong teeth tear food by jaw movements up and down, as their mouth and jaws cannot make side-to-side motion.

Cats occasionally chew grass — maybe to gain some extra fibre in their digestive system. (Or another theory opines that it helps prevent cat constipation.)

Fulltime indoor cats, perhaps in a high-rise apartment, don't have access to grass when the urge strikes. But some enterprising pet shops sell handy pottles of growing grass, so Puss can chew on this whenever the whim kicks in. If it's kept watered, the grass keeps growing for some time, pesticide-free. Also available are pottles of growing catnip — as a special party treat for the indoor cat.

Cats are strictly carnivorous, apart from the occasional nibble at some grass, but sometimes for their own mystic reasons they do take a bite out of other greenery. This is not always a good idea. Many plants are severely toxic to cats, causing serious distress. Those most likely encountered in the domestic garden would be hyacinths, belladonna, azaleas, asparagus fern, hydrangeas, foxglove, anemone, daffodils and poinsettia.

Veterinary surgeon and feline behaviourist Francesca Riccomini explains that when a cat becomes accustomed to one kind of pet food, which for some household reason is later changed to something different, the cat is likely to reject it. While this has a ring of 'cat being pernickety', there is a word which, without approving the behaviour, at least describes what the cat is suffering from: neophobia — 'fear of the new'.

At various times, prepared cat-foods (based on beef, chicken and fish) have been given rather imaginative names: Upstream Dream (salmon); Deep Sea Delight (mackerel); Cluck-a-Doodle-Doo; Fillet Meow; Hook-Line-and-Sinker; Sardines on Rice; Meow Sushi; and Kitty Pizza.

Polydactylism (from Greek 'many fingers') is a mutation which occurs in humans, but sometimes occurs in cats, too. They can be born possessing more than the usual number of toes. The usual number is five on each front paw and four on the hind paws, but extra toes sometimes occur on both front and hind paws.

Hair

Cats normally have four kinds of hair: down, awn, guard and vibrissae. *Down* hair is thin, short and soft, and sits closest to the cat's body as insulation. *Guard* hairs are the protecting top coat, longer and thicker in structure than *down*, and are arranged so that the underlying coat is kept dry. The *awn* hair grows between the *down* and *guard* hair, and is slightly more bristle-like. *Vibrissae* are the whiskers — longer and tougher hairs than those in the rest of the coat.

The precise colouring of a Siamese cat depends less on its parents than on the climate in which it grows.

Cats can sweat — but only through their paws.

When scents waft in through a cat's open mouth, they are received on the roof of the mouth by the highly sensitive 'Jacobson's organ', which conveys the scents' messages to the brain. Using this, one cat can detect another cat from as far away as 100 metres.

Because it lacks a true collarbone, a cat can take very long steps, curl its front legs, navigate its body through surprisingly small gaps, and crouch close to the ground's surface.

Purring

Various explanations have been put forward as to *how* cats purr, but nobody knows for sure.

Drs Sarah Ellis and Oliver Burman, from the University of Lincoln, used sophisticated electronic equipment to analyse two noticeably different purr-styles of the domestic cat.

Both scientists realised that most cat-owners would recognise and understand the two main sounds, to which they gave the formal definitions of: (1) a 'non-solicitation purr', expressing contentment, calmness and a relaxed frame of mind; and (2) the 'solicitation purr', when the cat lets it be known that it *wants* something.

But comparing the sound waves of both kinds of purr with existing attention-getting sounds from other sources, the two scientists made a surprising discovery: that the faster sound waves of (2) contained 'peaks' which were on a similar frequency to the cry of a baby — a sound to which humans are very likely to respond and find difficult to ignore!

Cats' larger relatives, such as lions and tigers, cannot purr properly.

The Scottish Fold cat is the result of an aberration which was continued by careful breeding: the cats' ears curl over onto their head, and look 'folded'.

Re-phrasing Rudyard Kipling, Dr Fogle sums up the cat's attitude and behaviour vey succinctly: *The cat marches to its own drumbeat.*

Instinct

British veterinary surgeon, author and popular TV broadcaster, the late Dr David Taylor, specialised in caring for zoo animals (including a killer whale in captivity!). His many books include studies of pandas, ponies, elephants, rabbits, hamsters, guinea pigs, dogs ... and the domestic cat.

Taylor's book *The Secret Life of Cats* describes that cats can feel earthquakes coming, and that the technique of those who hunt outdoors mirrors that of their relative, the jungle tiger. Taylor explains that the distance between the moggy's fang teeth is adapted to deal 'lethal dislocation' of live prey. Scratching furniture, he explains, is not always an exercise to sharpen their claws, but often to mark territory, exemplifying cats' attitude: 'What's mine, I scratch — French furniture upholstered in antique tapestry not excepted (nor contemporary naugahyde, nor sleek leather).

Taylor also explains that cats can produce over 30 different communication sounds, including 19 different 'miaows'; can sleep up to 16 hours out of 24; synthesise their own vitamin C so they don't need fruit and veg, and possess ears that have 30 muscles with 40,000 nerve fibres linked to the brain.

Furthermore, veterinarians have reported to Taylor that cat appointments are often cancelled by the owners, because on the day of the appointment the cats simply vanish. They just *know*.

Gwen Bailey, former Head of Animal Behaviour for the Blue Cross, explains that with a cat 'loyalty to a family' is less likely than with a dog, although the cat will bond to a house and territory — and to the food provided there. If there's any glitch or disfavour in the food supply of the 'home' territory, the cat will seek alternative food next-door without a backward glance. She also points out, in *What is My Cat Thinking?*, that cats can start to purr when they are one week old, and, because purring is separate from breathing, they can purr continuously while inhaling and exhaling.

Magnets on a cat's collar which cause the (metallic) cat-door to open, can become a hazard if the cat walks too near anything else made of metal — to which the collar-magnet joyously clings, holding the cat there with it, until released.

Cat age

How old is your cat in human terms? Nobody knows for sure, it's all guesswork. A persistently believed estimate that one cat year equals seven human years has been debunked by an alternative version which puts forward that:

- 👁 a cat at 1 year old is equivalent in maturity to a 15-year-old human

- 👁 at 2 years old, a cat has the same command as a 24-year-old person

- 👁 after the cat is 2 years old (and thus equivalent to 24 in human terms), for each year of the cat's life add 4 years of 'human equivalent'.

So when the cat is 6 years old it is '40'; at 10 years old it is '56'; and if the cat gets up to 16 it is the equivalent of '80'.

Sleep

Cats sleep on an average between 14 and 18 hours a day. A 15-year-old cat may have spent up to 10 years sleeping.

Ragdoll is a cat breed originating in California during the 1960s. Its notable behaviour characteristic is to become totally limp in the arms of whoever holds it.

Cat litter

Cat litter is made up from any of the following: wood shavings, chaff, dried citrus peel, corncobs, wheat husks, recycled newspapers, and Fuller's earth (a kind of clay). These soak up moisture, and a blend of gentle chemicals cuts down smells. Cleaning the litter-box during pregnancy requires the most fastidious treatment, since the cat faeces in the litter can contain a minute parasite called *Toxoplasma gondii*, which can be hazardous to the unborn child. Disinfecting the litter-box after emptying, and thorough handwashing with antiseptic should be observed.

Before cat litter became a commercialised commodity, people used ashes, dirt or sand as cat litter when it was necessary to keep the pets inside. One day in January 1947, a neighbour of Edward Lowe in Michigan came to him asking for some sand to use as cat litter. Her sand pile was frozen so she had been using ashes, but they tracked all over her house. Instead of sand, Lowe gave her some clay called Fuller's earth, a set of clay minerals capable of absorbing their weight in water. She found it worked far better than sand or ashes.

So Edward Lowe made up Fuller's earth into 5 lb bags and called it 'Kitty Litter'. At first it had to be given away free, because nobody quite knew what it was. But success gradually grew, and by 1964 Edward Lowe Industries was America's top producer of cat-box filler.

He decided the best way for his business to continue after his death was to hand the running over to a management team funded by venture capitalists. The sale went through in 1990, with the company being renamed the Golden Cat Corporation. The sale was later estimated by the *New York Times* as being worth $200 million.

In appearance and behaviour, the hyena seems to suggest a relationship with dogs ... but is in fact more closely related to the cat family.

A small bell around a cat's neck has been a traditional way of warning songbirds that doom might be nigh. But some animal experts advise that a smart puss can learn to control a single bell ... so anyone wanting to protect their garden birds should put *two* bells on the collar.

Emotions

Aloof though they often seem, like any living creatures cats experience changes within their thought processes, known to humans as 'emotions'. Jeffrey Moussaieff Masson's book *The Nine Emotional Lives of Cats* examines behavioural research and the studies of international cat experts to explain a cat's aloofness — or its mischief and affection.

Masson reminds the reader that the presence curled up in front of the heater is the result of a long journey originating from a solitary jungle predator — a former lifestyle whose evolutionary remnants can be misinterpreted as narcissism, or selfishness, but in fact are related back to survival. Born with a highly selective sense of curiosity, they are resolutely firm about categorising what interests them; and if it does not, it is totally ignored — which is often perceived as indifference.

Is it fair to perceive cats as cold and aloof? Jeffrey Masson says not. He is able to group their behaviour into nine categories: narcissism, love, contentment, attachment, jealousy, fear, anger, curiosity and playfulness.

4
Idioms

Like a cat on a hot tin roof

Several hundred years ago, before there was any roof made of tin, cats in Britain learned to avoid the backstone (or bakestone): a large flat stone at the side of the fireplace, on which thin oat cakes and flat scones were baked. Seeking warmth, cats sometimes accidentally stepped on one — very briefly! Hence by 1683 people were remarking that anyone moving quickly was *as nimble as a cat on a hot bake-stone*. Within a couple of hundred years, the saying had become *'Her 'oppeth like a cat 'pon 'ot bricks.'*

From meaning just 'speedy', the meaning gradually broadened to refer to a person with frayed nerves, ill at ease, uncomfortable and jumpy. When the saying reached America in about 1900, the 'hot bricks' began to give way to a 'hot tin roof'. That version was sealed into immediate recognition in 1955 when writer Tennessee Williams used the expression as the title of his world-famous play.

Letting the cat out of the bag

A secret is revealed, a confidence is broken — *the cat is out of the bag*. The saying is believed to date back to an ancient fraud, and has been in use since the mid-eighteenth century.

The story goes that in earlier centuries when many people shopped at a market (rather than at a supermarket), a live piglet was a desirable purchase for a housewife with a family dinner in view. A vendor would offer a closed, wriggling bag from which squealing could be heard.

But — *caveat emptor* — if the vendor was dishonest, the housewife who innocently took home a squealing, wriggling bag could find a cat inside it (a cat being somewhat easier to come by than a piglet). Another housewife, more discerning, would demand to have the bag opened for viewing, before purchase. Either way, when the bag was opened the vendor's secret was a secret no longer — the cat was out of the bag.

A pig in a poke is closely related and is even older. Richard Hilles's *Common-place Book* (1530) advises: *'When ye proffer the pigge — open the poke.'* *Poke* was the old word for 'bag' (its modern descendants are 'pocket' and 'pouch'). Again, the cat hidden in its bag is being passed off as a pig. The aforementioned housewife who didn't look inside the bag until she got home discovered that the 'pig' she had been sold inside the 'poke' was no pig. She had been duped. Hence, a *pig in a poke* signifies that something has not been properly inspected before purchasing, and turns out to be of less value than was charged.

Pragmatically, either story is hard to believe — a cat inside a tied-up bag being passed off as a piglet. That a woman accustomed to shopping for a household would be too dumb not to recognise the difference between a pig's squeal and a cat's yowl seems naïve. But besides Hilles, there is other evidence that such deceptions did occur. Thomas Tusser's *Five Hundred Pointes of Good Husbandrie* (1580) advises:

> let wit beare a stroke,
> for buieng or selling of pig in a poke.

All cats love fish, but fear to wet their paws

Wanting something of value without wanting to take the trouble or risk to obtain it. The saying came into English in 1250 — *Cat lufat visch, ac he nele his feth wete* — and Chaucer uses it in 1384.

A cat can look at a king

The proverb originated in Ireland, based on the observation that by nature cats are not obsequious and are certainly not impressed with anyone's human status. Based on this, the proverb indicates that even the most important of people can be looked at by ordinary folk. The saying appeared in print in 1546 as *'A cat maie look on a king, ye know.'*

Cat's Cradle

Children play this by looping string over their fingers and making patterns with twists and turns of their hands. With luck, an established pattern can be passed over onto another child's hands ... and the display continues. While the string shapes can (with some imagination) represent a 'cradle', the association with 'cat' is not so straightforward. The game is ancient and its concept is spread far — differing cultures around the world play such games with string.

The sun is the connection with 'cat' in the game's name. The sun was seen as a cat-figure in ancient Egyptian times, constantly fighting the darkness, and the symbolical association between 'cat' and 'sun' gradually passed from

Egypt to other areas of the Northern Hemisphere. In some areas, the game of twisting and shaping the string was aimed at controlling the sun. For instance, northern snow-bound cultures believed the string 'cradle' might make the sun captive, and thus bring sunshine to them for a longer time.

It is unlikely that modern children playing Cat's Cradle think they will have any influence on the movements of the sun, but that seems to be the ancient reason why the string 'cradle' is intended to hold a 'cat'.

(Another explanation also exists: that in parts of Europe a young married couple would celebrate the first month of their marriage by placing a real cat into a real cradle, which the two of them stood beside and gently rocked … and this ritual would assist the conception of a child.)

Cat's whisker

In the early 1900s, radio was not commonplace. But hobbyists and enthusiasts developed a system of tuning into distant 'wireless waves' with a small structure built around a natural crystal over which was stroked a thin, moveable wire — known as a *cat's whisker*. The cat's whisker was able to locate radio signals which had been picked up by an outdoor antenna and conveyed into the crystal. Once located, the rather frail sound was transferred into earphones. With a long antenna and a lot of luck, the cat's whisker could locate radio signals coming from as far as 40 kilometres away.

Pussy willows

A legend from Poland tells that centuries ago, when a mother cat's kittens were cruelly thrown into a river, the mother cat's meowing was so sad that the willow trees bent their branches down towards the water for the kittens to cling to and be saved. Ever since, willows near water have retained their 'weeping' stance.

Furthermore, the kittens and their mother cat, frightened to return to the house where they had been so cruelly treated, took refuge within the willows' branches and remained there, safely. The trees were so impressed with the gentle beauty of the tiny kittens, and the devotion of their mother, that they diligently protected them — and came to wish that they, too, could have little kittens of their own. So they put out catkins covered with fine grey fur — the willow version of Mother Puss's kittens. And the spirit of Nature decreed:

> 'Willow fair, dear willow fair
> Silver-gray pussies shalt thou bear,
> Because thy heart is kind and true,
> This thy wish I grant to you.'

The *Oxford Dictionary*, ever pragmatic, decrees otherwise:

> Any willow with soft fluffy catkins
> appearing before the leaves.

Bell the cat

The expression *to bell the cat* comes from Aesop's *Fables*, approximately 550 BC.

Some mice are having difficulty seeking food because of the danger from a nearby watchful cat. The mice hold a gathering in order to plan a defence strategy. One mouse puts forward the suggestion that a little bell could be placed around the cat's neck or tail, to warn the mice that the cat is coming near. But one wise old mouse comes forward to ask which mouse present will be the brave one who hangs the bell on the cat.

The idea of actually 'belling a cat' was not really novel — in order to protect songbirds in gardens, cats have been belled for many years. But for a mouse to actually hang the aforementioned bell was James Bond territory — which is what the expression has come to mean: undertaking a dangerous and risky project to disadvantage evil, and to benefit mankind.

Alley cat

An *alley cat* is a city-dwelling stray or homeless cat, with a tough disposition, a firm level of self-preservation and a somewhat elastic set of morals. The term is also often applied to a person of similar qualities — and is not a compliment.

The *alley* portion probably evokes the image of prostitutes, who used to lurk in alleys, sometimes carrying their own mattresses. The *cat* probably alludes to the take-on-all-comers habits of female cats when they are in mating mood.

Not enough room to swing a cat

The English language is such a polyglot, and has so much imagery coming into everyday use from widely differing sources, that quite often rival explanations develop about exactly where and how an expression arose. This is one of them: like distant family claiming a celebrity, five different sources lay claim to be the ancestor of *'no room to swing a cat'*.

Explanation 1

The most usually accepted is that the 'cat' referred to isn't a cat at all, but is the whip used for punishment in the old sailing-ship days: the dreaded cat-o'-nine-tails. When wielded on a misbehaved sailor's back, the whip's thongs provided a most painful experience. But to effect this, the whip's swinger needed room   more than the average ship cabin provided. So whippings were customarily carried out on deck, not only to demonstrate to the rest of the crew the consequence of evil ways, but also because the space on deck allowed room to 'swing a cat', which the cabin did not.

There is, however, some doubt about this explanation, because of the belief that 'no room to swing a cat'

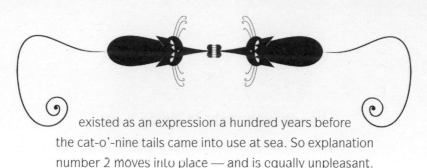

existed as an expression a hundred years before the cat-o'-nine tails came into use at sea. So explanation number 2 moves into place — and is equally unpleasant.

Explanation 2

That cats had mysterious and evil powers associated with witchcraft and should be tortured and killed was a rampant belief at roughly the same time as the battles within Europe required expert archers. As practice for archers, people actually did swing a cat and the archer tried to hit it with an arrow. An activity which obviously need a lot of space. If the cat wasn't literally swung by its tail (a little dangerous for the swinger, when facing a less-than-adept archer) it could be put into a sack or leather wine-container, hung from a branch, and then set swinging.

Shakespeare refers to it in *Much Ado About Nothing* (1598) when Benedick says: *'Hang me in a bottle like a cat and shoot at me ...'*. In 1850, Charles Dickens seems to favour a similar concept. In *David Copperfield*, when the character of Mr Dick uses the term, he appears to mean quite literally a cat being swung: *'You know, Trotwood, I don't want to swing a cat. I never do swing a cat.'*

Explanation 3

Back to sea for adherents of explanation number 3, who affirm that in this case *cat* is a corruption of *cot*, a shipboard term describing a form of hammock ... which needed space to be hung properly.

Explanation 4

Explanation number 4 remains with the sea, where the term *cat* can describe a compact merchant vessel. If a mooring did not have enough space for such a vessel to manoeuvre, then *there was not enough room to swing a cat*.

Explanation 5

Finally there is explanation number 5, which says that in certain Scottish dialects, *cat* means 'rogue', who when he runs out of luck will come to his end with a noose, the hanging of which needs a certain amount of room.

At least, amid the various tangles of its ancestry, the meaning of the expression has remained comfortingly stable and clear: *no room to swing a cat* is undoubtedly referring to a small area.

Cat-lap

Cat-lap is the scornful name for a 'soft' or non-alcoholic drink, something mild which a cat might lap, such as weak tea. A youth might be described as not yet old enough to drink anything except cat-lap. Sir Walter Scott mentions it in *Redgauntlet:* *'A more accomplished old woman never drank cat-lap.'*

Rub someone the wrong way

To irritate or upset a person: the reference is to cause annoyance to a cat by stroking its fur backwards.

To get one's back up

Showing anger or annoyance: the allusion is to a cat, which arches its back upwards (apparently to make itself look bigger) when threatened by a dog or other perceived threat.

There are more ways to kill a cat ...

The earliest known manifestation of such an idea appeared in John Ray's book *A Collection of English Proverbs* in 1678, and was actually about a dog: *'There are more ways to kill a dog than hanging.'* Over the centuries the image changed to a cat — and the ways of killing started to vary. By Charles Kingsley's time, in *Westward Ho!* (1855), Kingsley had it as *'There are more ways of killing a cat than choking it with cream.'* Variations have cropped up all along the way, such as using butter or pudding. And during the nineteenth century in America a variation crept in, concerning *skinning* a cat. Mark Twain in *A Connecticut Yankee in King Arthur's Court* (1889) has: '*she was wise, subtle, and knew more than one way to skin a cat.*' The basic intention of all the expressions seemed to be to point out that there can be several ways of accomplishing a desired object.

But in America the term *skinning a cat* has at least two other connotations. It describes a gymnastic exercise: hanging from hands on a tree branch or cross-bar, then drawing the feet and legs up through the arms and hauling the bodyweight upwards to finish sitting on the horizontal. (An effect to the viewer somewhat like skinning a creature!)

But the main American claimant to being the expression's ancestor is not a cat, but a fish. Unlike most other fish, a catfish, which has whiskers, needs to be skinned (not just scaled) before it can be cooked and eaten. Among communities which catch and eat their own fish, various groups have different ways of skinning their catch, which they customarily refer to as just a 'cat' rather than 'catfish'. But considering that the basis of the expression dates back at least to 1678, the application to fishing might be add-on rather than origin.

At least amidst the language confusion there is some comfort in the fact that none of it involves actually skinning a real cat.

A scorched cat fears even a cold stove

The cat has learned a lesson from not always applying wisdom correctly, then becoming overly cautious as a result. There are various versions: the earliest sighting in English being 1611 (*The scalded cat fears cold water*), and there is a similar concept in an Arabic saying: *A cat bitten once by a snake dreads even rope.*

Make the fur fly

This refers to a disturbance or altercation — not necessarily physical, but certainly spirited. Some think the saying developed from the 1890 nursery poem 'The Duel' by Eugene Field – which doesn't actually mention fur flying but certainly conveys a similar image, as in this excerpt:

> The air was littered, an hour or so,
> With bits of gingham and calico,
> While the old Dutch clock in the
>   chimney-place
> Up with its hands before its face,
>
> For it always dreaded a family row!
>
> ... But the gingham dog and the calico
>   cat
> Wallowed this way and tumbled that,
> Employing every tooth and claw
> In the awfullest way you ever saw—
> And oh! how the gingham and calico flew!

Note that sometimes the expression moves away from fur to 'making the feathers fly'.

You don't have a cat-in-Hell chance

This is a contraction of the original, slightly longer version: *No more chance than a cat in Hell without claws*. Either way, it has developed a strong image of a situation being hopeless without proper weapons of survival. Dropping reference to the 'weapons' in the shortened version doesn't seem to make much difference — surely the poor cat would be doomed anyway.

A modern version of the expression brings a more ominous note: *No more chance than a wax cat in Hell* ...

Look what the cat dragged in

A rather derogatory comment on someone's arrival. An obvious reference to cats' tendency to bring home its tattered and torn prey, after having 'played' with it for a while.

To live a cat-and-dog life

To be always arguing. If not coined by Thomas Carlyle, it was spread abroad by him in his 1865 book *Frederick the Great*: '*There will be jealousies and a cat-and-dog life over yonder worse than ever.*'

Putting the cat among the pigeons

The expression has its origin in an unfortunate truth: during the time of the British Raj, soldiers in India between military duties had to find ways of occupying their time. Sometimes they used to trap wild cats, and put them in a caged area with a lot of pigeons — then take bets on how many birds

the cat could swipe dead. Hence, *cat among the pigeons* —
meaning to cause trouble and make a stir, often by revealing
a controversial fact.

Grin like a Cheshire cat

Alice in Wonderland was intrigued when
she met a Cheshire cat who could fade
into invisibility until only its grin was left.
But author Lewis Carroll didn't invent
the expression about the grinning cat; it
was known over a century earlier, and is
mentioned by Peter Pindar (pen-name of
John Wolcott) in his *Lyric Epistles*, 1792.

Four centuries before that, a notorious
British swordsman called Caterling was
nicknamed the Cheshire Cat because he grinned broadly
when slaughtering anyone, so a person who grinned widely
was sometimes called ' a Cheshire Caterling', which later
abbreviated to 'a Cheshire Cat'. As defined in a 1788
Dictionary of the Vulgar Tongue: *'He grins like a Cheshire cat'*
— said of any one who shows his teeth and gums in laughing.

But most famously, the cheeses of Cheshire were often
made in a circular shape, with a cat's face imprinted on
them, and the curved shape made the cat's face appear to
be grinning.

So by 1865, Lewis Carroll had several reasons for making
his grinning cat come from Cheshire.

All cats are grey in the dark

Not just cats, of course — everything else in the dark is also grey; thus when the lights are out, appearances are meaningless. But cats in the dark have been the symbol of the concept since the proverb surfaced in 1546: *When all candels be out — all cats be grey...*

A bag of cats

It doesn't take much effort to imagine the result of putting several cats into one bag, hence the Irish expression '*bag of cats*' — referring to any situation which is noisy and bad-tempered: perhaps just one person in an ugly mood; a gathering which is out of control and turning rebellious; or a political party not noted for its calm behaviour — which is how the term is used in James Joyce's *Dubliners* (1914).

I'm so nervous — I'm having kittens ...

A human person described as 'having kittens' is in a state of serious upset. But why kittens? Why not puppies or baby crocodiles? The expression dates back to medieval times, when some women were thought to be witches. Thus, if another woman annoyed a 'witch', the witch could cast a spell over that woman's pregnancy and replace her baby with kittens. Then even the normal pangs of childbirth could be interpreted as the internal clawing of cats' claws — causing dramatic anguish in the labouring woman. Naturally any woman persuaded into the belief that she was bewitched and about to give birth to a litter of kittens would become hysterical with fright, so it is easy to see how the conviction that one was going to give birth to kittens came to mean a state past apprehension into panic.

In later centuries, the term crossed beyond women who were pregnant, and referred to anyone — even men — whose level of calm was being attacked.

Cat burglar

The term has been in use since the early 1900s, and refers to a burglar who can enter premises, and steal and depart without any noticeable noise — like a cat entering and leaving a room. If entry to the property to effect a burglary requires adept climbing and some athletics, the similarity to a cat is even more pronounced.

In the 1955 movie *To Catch a Thief*, Cary Grant played a retired burglar who had been known as 'The Cat', and Brigitte Auber played a younger and still-active 'cat burglar'.

Scaredy cat or fraidy cat

These two terms appear to have originated concerning a cat's turn of speed rather than any lack of courage. A cat will hiss, arch, 'puff up' and defy even quite a big dog. But when the same cat recognises genuine danger which cannot be dissolved by bluffing, it will escape with alacrity. Cats certainly are not cowards, but they are definitely smart enough to scamper away — often up the nearest tree — when a larger enemy threatens them. Their (perfectly sensible) practice of doing so has resulted in the rather unfair terms *fraidy cat* and *scaredy cat*. Those descriptions, referring to timidity, have been in use since at least 1900, and appeared in the poem 'Moo Cow Moo' by Canadian poet Edmund Vance Cook, in 1903.

Fat cat

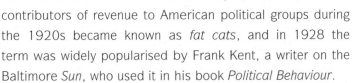

The term *fat cat* is used to describe a rich and influential person, plus suggesting associated imagery of self-importance, self-indulgence and probable laziness. This may not be entirely fair, since a real cat could have become fat because of being loved and cared for. Nevertheless, contributors of revenue to American political groups during the 1920s became known as *fat cats*, and in 1928 the term was widely popularised by Frank Kent, a writer on the Baltimore *Sun*, who used it in his book *Political Behaviour*.

Since then the expression has broadened its application and has increased in its 'put-down' quality. Besides politicians and their rich supporters, it is now often being applied to business people and administrators who are perceived as taking the 'cream' by disadvantaging the workers.

Raining cats and dogs

In ancient Northern Europe mythology, the gods of Nature were believed to be accompanied by animals. Odin, the Scandinavian god of war who was master of the winds, was surrounded by wolves and dogs. And the ungodly — the evil spirits, such as witches — were believed to be accompanied by cats, and rode on the gusts of storms. Thus, during severe wind and tumultuous rain, the mythological belief was that the dogs of wind had come out in full cry, chasing the cats of the evil spirits, who transformed themselves into rain to escape.

The belief was heightened by the feel of strong rain (when it hits you, there is a faint sting like a little scratch) and the sound of thunder (loud, sudden, often several explosions in succession — somewhat like the barking of a huge dog).

The above explanation satisfies most language scholars. But other folk-beliefs have also persisted. In 1652 playwright Richard Brome wrote the line *'raining dogs and polecats'*, but without explaining why. It has been construed as referring to the fact that in ancient towns the poor drainage facilities and rudimentary gutters meant that all kinds of filth, moving and still, were exposed to public view. After a big storm, the aforementioned gutter filth could contain the corpses of half-starved stray cats and street-living dogs. Such is

mentioned by the famous author Jonathan Swift, who wrote of it in 1710:

> Now from all parts the swelling kennels flow,
> and bear their trophies with them as they go . . .
> drowned puppies, stinking sprats, all drenched
> in mud, dead cats, and turnip-tops, come
> tumbling down the flood.

This seems a straightforward description of debris floating in a gutter, without any mention of where the debris originated. It is hardly sufficient to be the provenance of a long-lived expression, even if the more gullible among the citizens believed the bodies in the gutters had fallen from the sky — that it had literally been raining cats and dogs. (Although presumably the starving street-life animals also died and were seen in the gutters during non rainy periods.)

Or another version claims that cats and dogs tended to live up within the thatching of roofs, and during rain and wind ... fell out!

In 1738, over 20 years since his first reference to the puppies and cats in the gutters, Jonathan Swift wrote the phrase in the form we now know it: *'raining cats and dogs'*. Scholars would like to think he was connecting with the truly ancient mythology belief that connected wind with dogs, and rain with cats.

The cat's pyjamas

During the 1920s a wide collection of bizarre 'approval' expressions arose, by attaching nonsense attributes to animals: the eel's ankle, the oyster's garter, the snake's hips, the canary's tusks, the flea's eyebrows, the sardine's whiskers, the kipper's knickers, the elephant's instep, the bee's knees … and *the cat's pyjamas*. They were not intended to be taken seriously; they are simply an exclamation referring to something of rare quality: outstanding and to be admired.

Of these nonsense expressions, the cat's pyjamas may have had a fragile basis in fact. It is believed (but not proven) that during the late 1700s there was a London tailor called E. B. Katz who specialised in making luxurious silk garments, including pyjamas — Katz pyjamas — for royalty and other wealthy patrons.

But other writers believe *the cat's pyjamas* and *the cat's meow* originated in American girls' schools around the beginning of the twentieth century.

Putting aside the exact origin of the expression, there certainly is evidence for how the term *cat's pyjamas* became widely popularised. Tad Dorgan, an American sportswriter and cartoonist used the phrase freely and is credited with bringing it to a wider public. He is also credited with either inventing or popularising the term *hot dog*.

To sit in the catbird seat

Catbirds are American, related to mocking birds, and like their relatives are capable of a wide variety of imitative sounds — including a credible imitation of a mewing cat, hence their name.

Apparently the catbird likes to do its singing when perched on the highest possible location; safe from enemies and commanding a fine view. Thus arose an image of the *catbird seat* as being an advantageous place to be, and the expression began being used by American poker players, and then sports broadcasters, to describe a player who appeared to be in a particularly fortunate situation. In 1942 a mention of the phrase by James Thurber in a short story brought the phrase to greater prominence. With or without having actual advantages, the current application of *in a catbird seat* seems to be 'in a position of ease'.

Cat's paw

Apart from the obvious — the paw of a cat — the term *cat's paw* is heard as a put-down, describing a person who has been used by someone else to do their donkey work: a dupe, a pawn, a sucker. The expression dates back to a distant fable about a wily monkey watching some chestnuts roasting in embers. Although the chestnuts reached perfect roasted readiness, the monkey was unwilling to retrieve them and risk his own paws in the heat. A passing cat was waylaid by the monkey, and asked to draw the chestnuts from their red-hot bed. Uncharacteristically obliging (and stupid), the cat obliged, receiving burnt paws for its trouble — while the monkey enjoyed the nuts!

So we have the image of a person facing a foolish or even dangerous situation which they want turned to their advantage, then organising that the dirty work be done by someone else who thinks they're being helpful — a cat's paw.

(See also **Cats at sea.**)

A cat has nine lives

The myth that cats have nine lives has been around for centuries. It can be seen in Heywood's *The Proverbs of John Heywood* in 1546, and soon after in William Baldwin's *Beware the Cat* (1553, published 1561). Shortly after that, Shakespeare mentions it in *Romeo and Juliet* (c.1594). Tybalt asks Mercutio *'What wouldst thou have with me?'*, and Mercutio replies: *'Good king of cats, nothing but one of your nine lives.'*

The truth is that cats do not have nine lives — just one, like every other living creature. However, cats are particularly good at surviving disasters with the one life they have. They are small, quick-thinking, lightweight, fast and flexible, and have excellent balance. But the association of cats with nine lives existed long before it crept into the English language.

Ancient Egypt revered the cat, not only because they regarded it as having god-like qualities, but also because it was a practical beast and killed rats. And the Egyptians noticed, of course, that the cat could escape from tricky situations, and could survive falls and accidents. Thus they reasoned that it had more lives than just the usual one. Ancient Egyptians were also keen on numerology, and the number three had significance to them, as it still does to many cultures. Anything 3 x 3 was of even greater importance, so it was honouring the cats to declare that they possessed 3 x 3 lives: 9.

This belief that cats had nine lives inevitably drifted out from Egypt; it is mentioned in Arabic and Indian fables in the eighth century.

In addition, ancient Egyptians weren't the only people to find significance in certain numbers. The number nine has been a mystical and religious symbol for centuries. The Christian faith is based upon God represented in a trinity: Father, Son and Holy Spirit. Nine is a trinity of trinities. The Nordic god Odin gave his female counterpart Freja absolute rule over nine worlds. Some people believe that Jesus died on the cross during the ninth hour. Even in modern times, the figure nine has all sorts of images hovering about it in our consciousness: nine holes of golf; a cat-o'-nine-tails; nine-pins for bowling; *Deep Space Nine*; duration of pregnancy in months; Dante's 'nine circles' of Hell; Cloud Nine; the whole nine yards; dressed to the nines. So it's not surprising that the concept of *nine lives* has a ring to it and always did have.

Besides the athleticism of cats, and the various resonances of the figure nine, the belief that cats had nine lives got tangled up with the medieval European belief in witches, so that the myth grew that witch-women could change themselves into their pet cat, a total of nine times. While that concept faded away, the belief (or at least the expression) remains in the English language and the English-speaking psyche: that we have only one chance at life — but cats have nine.

Catty-corner

The term is widely used in America to mean 'diagonal', but, when asked, most people are flummoxed about what the connection could be between cats and a diagonal corner. The answer: there is no connection. *Catty-corner* has nothing to do with cats. The expression derives from the French word *quatre* meaning 'four'. In the Southern states of the United States this French word developed a dialect pronunciation (and spelling) as *'cater'*, so *cater-cornered* meant simply 'four-cornered', and was first seen in the 1880s. It could have stayed like that, but a custom arose whereby a diagonal position was described as *'cater-corner across'*. This became shortened to *cater-corner*, which then underwent a subtle change, because its sound reminded people of cats, and the word became *catty-corner*, or sometimes *kitty-corner*. But only in America — saying it elsewhere can get a puzzled reaction.

Cats and dogs

In the 1880s, *cats and dogs* was an American slang term on the stock market, referring to speculative stocks and shares of doubtful value or suspicious history.

Fight like Kilkenny cats

There is no substantial reason for believing that cats in the Irish county of Kilkenny are any more bellicose or aggressive than cats anywhere else. But at least two legends persist in trying to convince us that the cats of Kilkenny are lightweight champions of the world.

The illusion can be dated back to 1798 — a rebellious year

in Ireland, when foreign soldiers were garrisoned there. Bored with guard duties, it is believed that the soldiers would tie two cats together by their tails, then throw them into a 'fighting area' and watch the (very lively) battle. An addition to the basic story is that one day an officer was spied approaching, and a quick-thinking soldier drew his sword, severed the two tails, let the cats escape, and told the officer the cats had eaten each other and left only their tails!

But setting aside the sadistic soldiers, the fighting 'cats' may be referring to men. During the seventeenth century, the residents of Irishtown and Kilkenny had a bitter argument over the boundaries, and their persistent battling was compared to the fighting of cats.

There is no proof for any of the stories, but, regardless, the cats of Kilkenny have been left with a reputation for fighting with complete and utter determination right to the bitter end, in all-out conflict which no one can win. A folk poem helps keep the belief alive:

> There once were two cats from Kilkenny,
> Each thought there was one cat too many,
> They fought and they fit,
> And they scratched and they bit,
> Till excepting their nails,
> And the tips of their tails,
> Instead of two cats,
> There weren't any.

When the cat's away, the mice will play

Without supervision, some people misbehave. The ancient Romans knew it as *Dum felis dormit, mus gaudet et exsilit* (When the cat falls asleep the mouse rejoices). The saying drifted into French as *Ou chat na rat regne* (Where [there] is no cat, the rat reigns), and came into English during the fifteenth century: *When the cat is abroade the mise will play*.

It turns up in Shakespeare's *Henry V* (1599) when Westmoreland refers to '*playing the mouse in absence of the cat*'.

The Scottish version has a particular charm:

> Well kens the mouse
> When the cat is out of the house.

Cat's brains

Doesn't refer to the moggy intellect: it's the name geologists give to a mixture found in Nature — sandstone with chalk veins.

Walk the cat back (or walk back the cat)

Not a commonly used expression, but it surfaced in the United States during the 1980s. It refers to casting the mind back and assembling a sequence of events which led to a particular situation, then analysing the initial reasons why the events happened and what they have led to. The term came into prominence in the *New York Times Magazine* during the 1994 investigations into CIA activities.

Nervous as a cat in a room full of rocking chairs

Like any other creature, cats don't like danger from an unpredictable source. It is not very likely that a room ever would be full of rocking chairs, but, if it were, there's no doubt a cat would be uncomfortable for two reasons. Being on the 'chair' seat would give a feeling of being unbalanced and no longer in control. Or, attempting to find a path across the floor, the cat might — Heaven forbid — be struck on the tail or elsewhere by a rampant plunging 'rocker'. Hence, although it might seldom happen in real life, this quaint expression summons an immediate image of worry, jumpiness and inability to relax.

Do it in a cat's paw

Again referring to the gentle (and often silent) ways in which a cat can go about its business. To *do it in a cat's paw* means to perform some project so discreetly that nobody is aware it is being done.

A cat in gloves catches no mice

Sometimes, to get a job done effectively, you can't be gentle and polite all the time. This saying originates in fourteenth-century France, and in 1578 appeared in English as *A cat gloved catches no mice*. It was later popularised by American statesman Benjamin Franklin in *Poor Richard's Almanac*.

To land on one's feet

A person who is unexpectedly lucky, maybe has frequent good fortune or manages to recover from a disadvantage and rise into a more favourable situation, has 'fallen on their feet'. It works on the observation that cats in free-fall have remarkable twisting powers and seem almost always to be able to land on their feet. Back in the fourteenth century, the expression read as *he will land on his legs*, but later the feet took over.

See which way the cat jumps

Both English and French have the saying '*See which way the wind blows*' (*Savoir d'où vient le vent*), meaning to wait until various factors have fallen into place before making a decision. Transferring the notion to cats is entirely logical, since cats can be very unpredictable.

The transition from 'wind blowing' to 'cat jumping' was established by the nineteenth century. You can find it in the *Universal Songster* in 1825:

> He soon saw which way the cat did jump,
> And his company he offered plump.

But the entry of the *cat jumps* phrase into the English language has a cruel history.

In the days when cats were considered totally expendable, their unpredictability was seen as an asset by sportsmen and marksmen practising their skill. In a game called 'tip-cat', the unfortunate creature would be placed up a small tree or on top of a medium-height pole. The sportsman was not permitted to shoot the cat while static on its perch, but only in motion. Some would align themselves to shoot where they thought the cat would jump — often without success. The smart operator, confident of his speedy aim and quick trigger, would wait to *see which way the cat jumped*, then aim and fire when it was in mid-air.

Hence came the image of waiting until a situation had progressed to the point where action would be advantageous … such as sharemarket investors interpreting a buying or selling trend before acting on it themselves. They are waiting *to see how the cat jumps*.

The cat who got the cream …

A self-evident description: a cat looking fulfilled and self-satisfied. There's also *the cat who got the canary* (bordering on smug or even guilty), or its variation: *a cat with feathers in its craw*, meaning either a capture well made, or caught with evidence of guilt.

Has the cat got your tongue?

This curious and supposedly encouraging remark to someone who is remaining silent has a grisly and unpleasant background. Centuries ago in areas known now as 'the Middle East', punishments for misdemeanours were more severe and horrific than those now familiar to the Western world. In some contexts then, it was common that a ruler could order a thief be punished by having his hand cut off, and a liar or traitor by having his tongue cut out. Since cats were more highly regarded than thieves or liars, the cut-offs were given to the ruler's pet cats as a treat. Therefore, if someone didn't speak, and was asked if the cat had got their tongue ... sometimes it was true.

Curiosity killed the cat

In its original form, this favourite admonition to nosey-parkers had no connection with being curious. The term has been known since the sixteenth century, when it started out as *Care kills the cat.* The meaning of 'care' in those days had more to do with worrying than with being looked after. Cats, it was deemed, were over-cautious and over-careful ... and such behaviour brought anxiety, poor health, and even death. People, as well as cats, could die from too much 'care'. And although the expression is referred to in Gilbert and Sullivan's *H.M.S. Pinafore* in 1878 ('*Once a cat was killed by care, Only brave deserve the fair*') a transition was taking place with that word 'care' — and it was eventually replaced with 'curiosity'.

Like herding cats

Cats don't herd. So this expression indicates that a proscribed activity is going to be filled with frustration and probable futility. Everyone involved will go in different directions and decline to co-operate with everyone else.

American technology firm Electronic Data Systems (EDS.com) created a very funny TV/cinema commercial showing gnarled, hard-living cowboys expressing their pride in the skill they have spent a lifetime achieving: herding cats. The commercial shows a great many cats being herded — but, genuine though they look, one has the conviction that these scenes were faked ...

5
History

Ancient Egypt

In ancient Egypt cats were worshipped as godly. Anyone killing a cat ran the risk of being killed themselves. The death of a family's cat had to be observed by the family going into full mourning and shaving off their eyebrows.

The corpse of the humblest pet was not just buried — it was embalmed, mummified, and buried with ceremony. In 1888 a cats' burial ground was uncovered at Beni Hassan in Egypt, and the mummified bodies of thousands of cats were revealed. To the horror of later archaeologists, nearly all the bodies were pulverised to be used as fertiliser in Britain. Only very few genuine mummified cats were kept.

The cat Bast was supreme goddess of ancient Egypt, and had such a powerful image that, soon after the birth of human babies, they were equipped with a pendant showing her image, and babies' arms were often tattooed with a similar image — encouraging Bast to keep a protective watch over the child. From the sacred cats kept in temples, a small amount of blood was often taken for injecting into a child, helping to prevent it from catching an infectious disease.

Ancient burial sites near Luxor in Egypt have disclosed a statue from the eleventh dynasty of a King of Hana (approximately 2000 BC). Sitting at the king's feet is a suitably imperious cat, named as 'Bouhaki'. This is thought to be the first example known in history of a cat having been given a name.

In Ancient Egypt there was a belief that by night the sun stored its rays in cats' eyes, for safekeeping. And in Oriental countries, there was a strong belief that a cat's nocturnal prowling and the glow in its eyes would scare away evil spirits ...

The earliest known depiction of a cat as a domesticated pet comes from a tomb in Egypt dated to 2600 BC. In the Tomb of Ti (who was a hairdresser to the royal family, and thus very much a VIP), there was found a small picture of a cat wearing a collar, suggesting that by then the cat was allied with the world of humans.

And although facts about Cleopatra are scarce, it is widely believed that she too had a pet cat (c. 30 BC).

A ceramic tile dating from Roman times showing the imprint of a kitten's paw was found in York, showing that cats have been in Britain for over a thousand years (and that kittens seeing wet clay, haven't changed ...).

Patron saint of cats

Gertrude of Nivelles was a seventh-century abbess in Belgium. She has a 'celebration day' on 17 March, and although never officially canonised, she is referred to as 'Saint' Gertrude and regarded as the 'patron saint' of gardeners, travellers, people with mental illness, and the recently deceased (on the first night of their perceived three-day journey to the next world). Legends about her also include her rather inexplicable ability to offer 'protection against rats and mice', which is often interpreted to make her 'patron saint of cats'.

Charles Lindbergh

In 1930, an issue of stamps in Spain featured famous aviators, including Charles Lindbergh who had flown from New York to Paris in 1927, in *The Spirit of St Louis*. Lindbergh often took his cat Patsy with him on flights, but on this New York–Paris flight he had decided not to, saying it was 'too dangerous a journey to risk the cat's life'. The Spanish 1-peseta commemorative stamp shows the plane taking off, with Patsy the cat sitting aground and wistfully watching the *Spirit of St Louis* becoming airborne — without her. (Lindbergh took a Felix toy doll with him instead of Patsy. See **Felix the Cat**.)

Dick Whittington's cat

A mystery. Although immortalised in a hundred storybooks and a thousand pantomime performances, it seems unlikely that Sir Richard Whittington's companion was an actual living, breathing cat. *Cat* in some contexts means a kind of boat — although alas, the term 'cat-boat' means different things to different people (see **Cats at Sea**). But certainly coal from Newcastle was being transported to London even before Whittington became mayor in 1397, and a 'cat-boat' was often used for transporting coal.

Whittington may have sent such a boat to the King of Barbary and had it return laden with riches. Or, as legend would have it, he may have sent a real cat, which cleaned up the mice in Barbary and earned the king's gratitude. (This version pre-supposes that the King of Barbary had never before met a cat ...). We'll never know, and perhaps it's best we don't. For if those who maintain Dick's 'cat' was actually a boat, many actors would be out of work in the pantomime season.

And even if Dick Whittington had a 'cat-boat' rather than an actual cat, the legend is powerful enough for there to be a memorial statue of Dick Whittington's cat, on Highgate Hill in North London, on the spot where reputedly Whittington heard the bells of Bow church tell him to return to London where he would three times be mayor. Indeed the real Sir Richard Whittington genuinely was three times Mayor of London — a statue of him in full mayoral robes stands outside the Royal Exchange in London. But if the London monument to Whittington's cat was replaced with a cat-boat, it wouldn't look as good.

British humorist Edward Lear at one time had a new house built. The builders were instructed to make the new dwelling an exact copy of the old one — so that the family cat would not be confused when they took up residence.

Cats and women

Why are cats associated with women? The interest generated by Egypt's goddess Bast (a female goddess with a cat head) lives with us still. Bast was goddess of motherhood, fertility, happiness and pleasure. Those factors sit easily on cats: they are normally good mothers, find luxury hard to resist, are adept at finding warmth and comfort, and — above all — epitomise beauty and graceful movement. Throughout history the same characteristics have been manifested by women.

Black cats

Black cats were popular long before they became associated with 'black magic', witches and sorcery. When that belief took hold, black cats were outlawed by the Christian church. But only completely black cats qualified as servants of the Devil; any with a touch of white somewhere were considered as not entirely belonging to Old Nick.

The slaughter of all-black cats caused them to become quite rare, and even today a tiny patch or sprinkling of white on an otherwise black cat is a reminder that this 'imperfection' was once vital to the creature's survival.

Florence Nightingale owned 17 cats at any one time — totalling over 60 during her life.

Cat shows

Cat-owners in England started organising 'showings' of their cats as early as 1861. Then in 1871 came the first official 'Cat Show' at the Crystal Palace, attracting 170 entries and hundreds of visitors and spectators. For the first time, 'entries' had to be in specific classes and standards; a system which has been practised worldwide ever since. By 1887 Britain had organised a National Cat Club, and 1893 saw the publication of the first official cat stud book — serious cat-breeding had begun. Currently the National Cat Show in London (the biggest in the world) attracts over 2000 pedigree entrants.

America had its first cat show in 1881; by 1895 the event had moved to Madison Square Garden.

A legend tells that, in the fifth century BC, the King of Persia ordered his army to attach live cats to the front of their shields, when attacking Egypt. The Egyptian soldiers, all cat-worshippers, were totally reluctant to wound the cats, and certainly not to risk killing them, and thus surrendered to the Persians. (Two other versions of the legend advise either that (a) each Persian soldier simply held a cat in one arm, or (b) cats were gathered together and released to run ahead of the Persian army into the battle area, causing considerable confusion among the Egyptians.)

Isaac Newton

Isaac Newton invented the reflecting telescope and created definitive work on the principles of motion, the discovery of calculus, and the principles of gravity.

He is also credited with inventing the cat door. Newton is reputed to have cut *two* 'doors' into his room: an adult-sized one for the cat — and a smaller one for her kittens. Which is rather odd, since Newton's knowledge of mathematics must have suggested that small kittens could easily go through the bigger door ...

Queen Victoria

The young Queen Victoria quickly established her support for the humane treatment of animals. She encouraged the Society for the Prevention of Cruelty to Animals and allowed them to add the 'Royal' to its name. When the RSPCA asked her permission to establish a Queen's Medal, Victoria noticed that no cat appeared among the animals on the submitted medal design — and she herself carefully sketched a cat into the group in the proposal drawing.

When Queen Victoria had a major celebration, such as a jubilee, there was a royal ritual of granting some jailed prisoners 'remission and release'. This required the Queen's signature. But if Victoria ascertained that any nominated prisoner had been convicted because of cruelty to animals, she refused to sign a release for him, describing such cruelty as 'one of the worst signs of wickedness in human nature'.

Ship's cat

British navigator Matthew Flinders mapped the coast of Australia in 1802, aboard the ship *Tryall*, accompanied by his remarkable black-and-white cat Trim. During the voyage, Trim learnt to swim and catch a rope. Together, they circumnavigated Australia three times and the world once. Flinders wrote the story of Trim and his voyaging in 1810, but it was not published until 1973. A bronze statue of Trim in one of Sydney's main streets was unveiled in 1996.

Albert Schweitzer, who was left-handed, occasionally chose to write with his right hand ... because his cat Sizi, for some perverse reason, liked to go to sleep sprawled across his left arm, and the good doctor declined to disturb her.

Pest control

Hywel Dda was Prince of Wales in the year 936. Realising that cats were an asset to pest control and therefore to agriculture in general, the prince set a range of prices for kittens and cats, and instituted punishments for their being stolen or killed. Prices varied according to a cat's age and whether it had established mouse-killing skills. Refunds were possible if a purchased cat proved lackadaisical in the mouse-killing department, or if a female showed no inclination to breed.

The Cat and Mouse Act

After the country of New Zealand allowed all adult women the vote in 1893, and Australia followed suit in 1902, the impulse for change spread worldwide. In Britain, women activists known variously as 'suffragists' or 'suffragettes' took up the cause with energy and diligence. Fearlessly they 'demonstrated' in public and made their voices heard, sometimes destroying property to draw attention, and frequently breaking the law. Naturally the result of this latter boldness was arrest and often imprisonment.

In prison, the suffragettes simply refused to eat The prisons responded by 'force-feeding' the unco-operative women, until public outrage caused this to be ceased. In 1913 the British Government found a way of dealing with the 'hunger-strikers', and introduced the Prisoners Temporary Discharge of Ill Health Act. Under this law, women in prison on hunger-strike who reached a point of dangerous weakness were discharged, but were subject to re-arrest to finish their prison sentence as soon as health was regained.

The comparison between a powerful government victimising women, and a cat 'playing' with a captured mouse, quickly resulted in the Prisoners Temporary Discharge of Ill Health Act becoming known as the Cat and Mouse Act. The expression 'playing cat and mouse' may well have been in use for many years before — but not attached to a specific law.

Britain allowed all adult women to vote in 1928.

In 1205, a Cistercian nunnery in Tarrant Kaines, in Dorset, England, did not require the nuns to wear hair-shirts, go barefoot or live on just grains and water ... They were allowed milk. One more amiable rule was: '*Ye shall not possess any beast sisters, except only a cat.*'

Saved by the cat

Sir Henry Wyatt (born 1460) was a supporter of the Tudors, and thus incurred the wrath of Richard III, who ordered that Wyatt be imprisoned. He was kept in squalor, was tortured and poorly fed. Legend has it that one day a cat appeared at his cell window, dragging a dead pigeon, which was left on the sill. Wyatt persuaded the gaol-keeper to cook the bird, and the cat continued to bring a pigeon for him every day. Thus sustained, Wyatt survived imprisonment, and on the death of Richard III was restored to freedom, grew rich and powerful, and was appointed guardian of the young prince who later became Henry VIII.

If the legend about the pigeons is true, one can only hope Sir Henry shared some of his later comfort with the cat who helped him survive to attain it.

There has been a rumour for centuries that Julius Caesar didn't like cats. We all know what happened to him.

Birman cats

Centuries ago, the cats known as Birman were sacred creatures in the Lao-Tsun temple of the Khmer people in Asia. In the early 1900s the temple was attacked by marauders, but the priests were helped to overcome the raid by two Western men: Auguste Pavie and Major Gordon Russell. As grateful thanks to the two men, in 1919 the priests sent them a pair of the precious Birman cats to France. The male cat did not live, but the female was pregnant — and from her, Birman cats became established in the West.

Siamese cats

When the British Consul to Siam, Owen Gould, was due to leave Bangkok in 1884, King Chulalongkorn (earlier tutored by Anna Leonowens when he was a boy prince) presented Gould with two Siamese cats as a farewell present. Up until then, Siamese cats were only ever owned by the royal family or the upper level of Thai aristocracy, and had never been seen in Britain. Gould's sister, Mrs Veley, exhibited the pair at the Crystal Palace in 1886, and cat fanciers fell in love with them immediately.

In old Siam, when a member of the royal family died, a tomb was prepared with a series of holes which eventually led from the casket to the outside air. A live Siamese cat was buried with the royal body — and when the cat eventually navigated its way through the complex of holes and emerged into the outside air (as it always did), the populace then knew that the royal soul had been released.

Cats in art

Leonardo da Vinci often sketched cats, in motion and at rest. He also made preparatory drawings for a study of *The Madonna and Child with Cat*. The final painting — if he ever finished it — has never been found, but the preparatory drawings survive. Rembrandt also combined the image of the Madonna and a cat, in *The Virgin and Child with Cat*.

The accepted wisdom is that cats as we know them were introduced to domestic society approximately 5000 years ago. But the German artist Albrecht Dürer swept such historic restriction aside when in 1504 he depicted *The Garden of Eden* ... showing a cat curled cosily around Eve's feet — in the year dot.

Historically, an unfounded vague perception of the cat representing evil or treachery is sometimes put forward as the reason why a cat appears in some depictions of Jesus' last supper: Ghirlandaio has a cat at the feet of Judas in 1480, Jacopo Bassano (1542) and Francesco Bassano (1586) both feature a cat under the supper table, and Tintoretto (1594) places a cat with the servants attending Jesus and the disciples.

6
Movies

Pussy Galore

The character of Pussy Galore was first introduced to the world by Ian Fleming in his 1959 novel *Goldfinger*. Pussy was leader of a criminal gang of lesbians called 'The Cement Mixers'. In the 1964 movie version of this James Bond story, Pussy was brilliantly portrayed by Honor Blackman.

Pyewacket

In 1644, after keeping a young woman without sleep for four days, British witch-hunter Matthew Hopkins extracted a confession from her that she was indeed a witch. Her 'familiars' were cats, dogs, a rabbit and a ferret, with names including Jamara, Ilemauzer, Griezzel and Pyewacket. Matthew Hopkins commented that these were names which 'no mortal could invent'. Nevertheless, with or without its history of supposed evil, Pyewacket became current as a name for a pet cat.

Three centuries after it was first noticed, the name Pyewacket was reunited with its 'witch' image in 1950 when John van Druten's hit play *Bell, Book and Candle* opened on Broadway, telling about a beautiful modern witch (Lilli Palmer) and her equally beautiful familiar, the cat Pyewacket. In 1958 the play became a movie starring Kim Novak.

After that, the name Pyewacket suggested beauty and intrigue rather than evil, and, besides naming many pets, it surfaces internationally as a catchy name for some high-class restaurants, an aristocratic racehorse, a rock group, a theatre in Chicago, and a luxury charter yacht.

Catwoman

The sleek figure of Catwoman was first seen in the 1940 magazine cartoons of Bob Kane, who had originated Batman in the Detective Comics a year earlier. She started out as a burglar and adversary of Batman, but Catwoman's character developed into a more sexy image and a possible romantic interest for Batman.

Besides magazine comic strips, Catwoman has been seen in both small- and big-screen movies, and in animation. She has been played by Julie Newmar, Eartha Kitt, Lee Meriwether, Michelle Pfeiffer and Halle Berry.

Cat Ballou

In a 1965 hit movie of the same name, Jane Fonda played Catherine Ballou, known as 'Cat' — a young schoolteacher setting out to avenge the murder of her father.

Cat People

Cat People was a 1942 horror movie (directed by the esteemed Jacques Tourneur) telling of a Serbian-born fashion artist in New York, carrying an ancient curse which caused her, when emotionally aroused, to turn into an avenging panther!

 Actor James Mason had a favourite cat called Flower Face.

That Darn Cat

Based on the book *Undercover Cat* by Gordon and Mildred Gordon, the 1965 movie *That Darn Cat* told the story of a wise cat working with top-ranking security agents to catch law-breakers. Hayley Mills and Roddy McDowall helped.

The Three Lives of Thomasina

Based on a book by Paul Gallico, this whimsical 1964 film was about a young girl's pet cat who died after attention from a veterinarian — but came under the influence of a beautiful contemporary witch who had skills at reviving the dead. Patrick McGoohan and Susan Hampshire starred.

Octopussy

Ian Fleming again. His short story 'Octopussy', published in 1966, had nothing to do with cats. James Bond is depicted up against the forces of evil, as usual, this time including a beautiful smuggler known as Octopussy. Maud Adams played the role in the 1983 movie.

Dame Maggie Smith

Dame Maggie plays Minerva McGonagall in the *Harry Potter* movies. In the first movie, *Harry Potter and the Philosopher's Stone* (2001), Dame Maggie's first appearance is as a cat who before our very eyes changes into Ms McGonagall, the senior staff woman of Hogwarts college for wizards, and who is able to turn herself into a cat at will — and indeed does so a couple more times in the same film.

Elizabeth Taylor's favourite cat had the
name Jeepers Creepers.

Rhubarb

The 1951 movie *Rhubarb* tells of an eccentric millionaire who
leaves his fortune, and ownership of a baseball club, to a
cat, Rhubarb. Alas, the club's publicist, and now Rhubarb's
guardian, has a fiancée who is allergic to cats …

Romeo and Juliet

A bizarre movie version of Shakespeare's
Romeo and Juliet was made in 1990,
featuring a cast made up entirely of cats. The
project took over a year to film, mainly on the
streets, and voices were supplied by an all-star
cast: Vanessa Redgrave, Ben Kingsley, John Hurt,
Dame Maggie Smith.

James Bond

A beautiful white cat called Solomon twice shared the silver
screen with Sir Sean Connery: in *You Only Live Twice* (1967)
and *Diamonds Are Forever* (1971).

 Hollywood film-maker Julia Phillips (author
of *You'll Never Eat Lunch in This Town
Again*) named her cat Caesar — so she
could call it Julia's Caesar.

Evil's cat

The Austin Powers movies tell us that Dr Evil spent 30 years suspended in space, and frozen. His re-entry to Earth went tolerably well — except that his cat was incorrectly thawed and as a result became bald. This plot twist is solved by the role of the cat, Mr Bigglesworth, being played by a hairless Sphynx.

The Incredible Journey

Scottish author Sheila Burnford's 1961 novel *The Incredible Journey* was an action adventure story about a bull terrier, a Labrador and a Siamese cat, who together trekked 480 kilometres across one of the wildest parts of Canada, searching for their masters. The story reached great popularity when filmed by Disney in 1963 as *The Incredible Journey*, and a second (animated) movie version followed in 1993 as *Homeward Bound: The Incredible Journey*, with Michael J. Fox, Sally Field and Don Ameche providing the voices for the three animals.

Over the years a public perception arose that the basic adventure was true ... overlooking that the 1961 original story was fiction.

Gay Purr-ee

The animated movie hit of 1962 told the story of the country cat Mewsette and her adventures when she comes to the big city. An all-star cast of voices included Judy Garland, Robert Goulet and Hermione Gingold.

The Aristocats

Disney again — an animated movie
in 1970. Eva Gabor provided the voice for
Duchess, the star character. Set in Paris
in 1910, the story tells how Duchess, a
beautiful pedigree cat, was kidnapped
to prevent her coming into a cat
fortune. The rough alley-cat Scat was
voiced by Scatman Crothers.

Lady and the Tramp

More Disney, in 1955. The first animated feature film in
CinemaScope, it told of a gentle spaniel who fell in with a
rough lot ... among whom were two mean Siamese cats
called Si and Am. Peggy Lee provided voices for both.

 **Movie star Warren Beatty's favourite cat
was called Cake.**

The Cat's Meow

Based on a 1997 play by Steven Peros, the 2001 movie
presents a semi-factual story of movie celebrities on a luxury
yacht, and the subsequent mysterious death of one of them –
millionaire Thomas Ince. In an early scene, as the celebrities
arrive, one character naïvely remarks how enjoyable the
cruise will be. But Thomas Ince, already noticing personality
cross-currents beginning to emerge, replies ironically: 'Yes –
the cat's meow.' Which became the play's – and the movie's
– title.

Josie and the Pussycats

This 2001 movie had nothing to do with real cats — its story was about an all-woman rock band with a provocative name, and is loosely based on the Archie comic and the early 1970s TV cartoon series of the same name.

Figaro

Italian writer Carlo Lorenzini (aka 'Collodi') created the story of Pinocchio in 1883, but there was no friendly Figaro character. Over 50 years later, the story was made into a wildly successful Disney movie (1940). But purists were not pleased. The movie had 'created' two new characters, which were not in Collodi's original story — Cleo the goldfish and Figaro the cat. Figaro, however, was such a hit with audiences that he went on to have many other appearances after the *Pinocchio* movie.

Breakfast at Tiffany's

Truman Capote's novella (1958) introduced the world to the whimsical young woman called Holiday 'Holly' Golightly (occupation: travelling) and her cat, called simply Cat. The movie (1961), starring Audrey Hepburn as Holly, featured a substantial marmalade-coloured cat as Cat. Utterly memorable though Audrey Hepburn was, no Oscar came her way — but the cat (real name, Orangey) won a PATSY award for his animal acting.

Actress Janet Leigh called her cat Turkey.

Patsy

The American Humane Society created the 'PATSY award' in 1939, and first awarded it in 1951, to recognise talented animals appearing in movies (Picture Animal Top Star of the Year/Performing Animal Television Star of the Year). By 1958 the decision was made to include television, and 1973 saw the first award for an animal in TV commercials: a cat named Morris for capturing television viewers' attention in advertising cat-food. Award-winners have included Orangey (for his role in the movie *Rhubarb*), Pyewacket (for *Bell, Book and Candle*) and Orangey again (for *Breakfast at Tiffany's*), Syn (for *That Darn Cat*), Midnight (for *Mannix*) and Tonto (for *Harry and Tonto*). The award has also been given to dogs, chimpanzees, dolphins, rats, lions and mules.

7
Cartoons

MAD-cat

Canadian television viewers were introduced to the clumsy bionic 'Inspector Gadget' in 1983. Through several television series, and later movies, the Inspector battled against the Malevolent Agency of Destruction and the evil Dr Claw, whose cat was known as MAD-cat.

Sylvester the Cat

He made his debut in a 1945 animated movie cartoon called *Live with Feathers*, then a follow-up episode called *Peck Up Your Troubles*. Sylvester quickly established the cry 'Suffering succotash!', and in 1947 became an Oscar winner, by which time the character of Tweetie-Pie the canary had joined the cast. From then on, Sylvester's main aim in life seemed to be catching Tweetie-Pie ... But through the following decades and two more Oscars, Tweetie Pie continued to escape. Besides 'Suffering succotash!' (*succotash*: a cooked mixture of corn kernels and lima beans), the series introduced two other concepts which charmed the public: the Mexican mouse named Speedy Gonzales, and the famous song '*I tawt I taw a puddy tat, a tweeping up on me ...*'.

Snagglepuss

This cat first appeared in cartoons in 1959 as a supporting character, but began in his 'own show' in 1961. Whenever he got in a fix, which was often, he yelled out 'Heavens to Murgatroyd!', which rapidly became a children's catch-cry among viewers, and is still occasionally heard now as an exclamation of big surprise.

Garfield

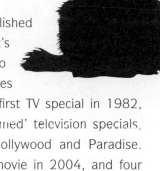

The first Garfield cartoon was published on 19 July 1978. Since then, the cat's philosophy has been compared to that of Nietzsche, Aristotle, Descartes and Jean-Paul Sartre. He had his first TV special in 1982, followed by 13 other Garfield-'themed' television specials, involving Christmas, Halloween, Hollywood and Paradise. He starred in his first full-length movie in 2004, and four other movies followed. A breed of marigold is named after the lasagne-loving cat — because it is the same colour as Garfield!

Arlene and Nermal

Arlene is Garfield's girlfriend. No shrinking violet, she argues with Garfield about his need to go on a diet, and agonises about her own need to have her teeth fixed. Circling around their lives is young Nermal, the self-proclaimed 'World's cutest kitten'. Garfield finds the kitten's conceit and self-confidence highly irritating.

Tom and Jerry

One of the most famous cat-and-mouse pairings in movie cartoons. Tom originally started out in 1939 being called Jasper, and the mouse had no name. Their first appearance was in 1939, in a short Hanna-Barbera cartoon called *Puss Gets the Boot*. In 1940 the cat was re-created by Chuck Jones as Tom, and started his frenetic pursuit of Jerry the mouse. Tom and Jerry continued their chase through 160 movie cartoons, winning seven Oscars. In 1965 their exploits began to be screened on television, and they starred in a full-length animated movie in 1993, as well as in videos and DVDs.

Associating the names Tom and Jerry actually began in 1821, when English sportswriter Pierce Egan wrote of a roistering pair of Londoners called Tom and Jerry, who were constantly in trouble, as published in *Life in London* and later produced as a stage play. An egg-nog-and-rum drink was named after them, and was still mentioned over a hundred years later, by Damon Runyon in *Dancing Dan's Christmas*. In 1957 the Tom and Jerry conjunction surfaced again as the title of a singing duo ... who later changed their name to Simon and Garfunkel.

Snowball

Marge and Homer Simpson lost their cat Snowball in a car accident. The moggy was replaced by ... Snowball 2nd. Daughter Lisa wrote an impassioned poem about the event:

> I had a cat named Snowball ...
> She died! She died!
> Mom said she was sleeping ...
> She lied! She lied!
> Why oh why is my cat dead?
> Couldn't that Chrysler hit me instead?

Felix the Cat

A cartoon character with a truly phenomenal impact. It started in 1919 when the cat figure emerged from the studio of entrepreneur Pat Sullivan, in an animated movie short called *Feline Follies*. Originally called Master Tom, his later name, Felix, was contrived as a combination of 'feline' and 'felicity' — which, since it meant 'happiness', was seen as an antidote to any lingering suspicious concern about black cats.

Such was Felix's success that within 10 years he appeared in 150 animated cartoons. His newspaper comic-strip debut in 1923 led to his appearing in over 200 publications worldwide, in many languages.

Felix's popularity grew enormously — besides featuring on a proliferation of toys, games, cards and jewellery, he was the first balloon in the Macy's Thanksgiving parade and was the mascot chosen by Charles Lindbergh on his famous flight across the Atlantic.

A 'Felix doll' was used in early American television experiments, and in 1930 Felix became the first image to be transmitted by NBC television. Over 200 episodes of Felix's adventures were shown and repeated on American television for 20 years. His first full-length movie, *Felix the Cat, the Movie*, played in rotation on the Disney Channel for 10 years, and 9 million 'Felix meals for kids' were sold in Wendy's fast-food chain.

In the twenty-first century, Felix began to enjoy an even greater popularity in Japan, with a new television series and the creation of a Japanese theatre musical. The early classic cartoons have been released on DVD, and enthusiastic celebrity fans include Ringo Starr, Whoopi Goldberg, Justin Timberlake, Cameron Diaz and the Dixie Chicks, while fashion publications featuring Felix include *Vogue*, *Cosmopolitan* and *Elle*.

Dennis the Menace

In 1976, Hank Ketcham's cartoon creation Dennis the Menace, told his mother: '*Meow is like "Aloha" — it can mean anything!*'

Calvin and Hobbs

This cartoon strip first appeared in 1985, and its popularity skyrocketed. Its circulation had reached syndication in 2400 individual newspapers by the time artist Bill Watterson 'retired' the two characters in 1996 and ceased drawing them. By then, 23 million *Calvin and Hobbs* books had been published. Six-year-old Calvin's companion Hobbs is actually a tiger ... but cartoonist Watterson confessed that the character was totally inspired by his grey tabby cat, Sprite.

8
Music and
songs

Pulcinella

Domenico Scarlatti had a cat called Pulcinella, who was curious about Scarlatti's harpsichord. The sounds of her walking on its keyboard were eventually developed by the composer into his *Cat's Fugue* (1739).

The Cat Waltz

Over a century later, Chopin was composing his Waltz No. 3 in F major, when his cat also scrambled across the keys of his piano. The composer included a version of the sounds into the waltz — known thereafter as Chopin's 'Cat Waltz' (1838).

'Kitten on the Keys'

In 1921 American composer Zez Confrey was staying at his grandmother's house and was woken in the middle of the night by strange sounds coming from the piano in the parlour. Stumbling downstairs, Confrey found granny's cat parading up and down the piano keyboard.

The incident became a famous 'novelty piano solo': 'Kitten on the Keys' (1921).

'Alley Cat'

Keeping up the good work, Danish composer Bent Fabricius-Bjerre (aka Bent Fabric) created the jaunty piano solo 'Alley Cat', which won a Grammy award in 1963 for 'Best Instrumental'.

Opera for cats

1983 saw the first performance of an unusual two-act opera by prolific German composer Hans Werner Henze (d. 2012) in which all the characters are cats — played by opera singers, appropriately costumed. Based on an original tale by Honoré de Balzac, *The English Cat* tells in music the bizarre story of a group of cats in Victorian London, who are not only vegetarian, but are also dedicated pacifists who believe that rats are treated badly, and that there should be a Royal Society For The Protection of Rats. So far the opera has not reached a consistent place in the popular repertoire.

Cats in love

Maurice Ravel's 'children's opera' *L'Enfant et les Sortilèges*, to a libretto by Colette, featured a duet between a male and female cat — regarded by scholars as being the first serious treatment in lyric music of cats' love.

The cats' duet

Rossini's 'Duet for Two Cats' is a crowd-pleasing showcase for two sopranos, elegantly recorded by two of the finest sopranos in history: Elisabeth Schwarzkopf and Victoria de los Angeles.

 John Lennon's pet cat was called Elvis.

Classical trivia

- Stravinsky composed *Lullabies for the Cat*.
- Prokofiev used a 'purring' clarinet to be the cat in *Peter and the Wolf*.
- Fauré mimics the frolicking of a kitten in 'Kitty Valse'.
- Tchaikovsky has a *pas de deux* for two cats in the ballet *Sleeping Beauty*.

'What's New Pussycat?'

Tom Jones's big hit in 1965. The song, composed by Burt Bacharach and Hal David, had little to do with cats — although described by one reviewer as 'an anthem for Las Vegas hepcats'. It was sung with Jones's usual impact and gusto as the title for a movie of the same name (starring Peter O'Toole and written by Woody Allen).

'The Pussycat Song'

In 1948 Bob Crosby was joined by Patty Andrews for a novelty song involving a serenading tomcat and his sweetheart, who has been locked inside the house ('*Come yeowt my purrdy pussy, we could serenade the moon—*' '*Not neeoww…*').

'I Bought Me a Cat'

Composer Aaron Copland's 1950 setting of an old folk song for children, taught to him by writer Lynn Riggs.

The Pirates of Penzance

No cats appear in this Gilbert and Sullivan icon, but they are not entirely forgotten. The pirates refer to them in the chorus:

> With cat-like tread,
> Upon our foe we steal
> In silence dread,
> Our cautious way we feel

... rendered comic in performance when sung by a dozen men in full voice with orchestral support — in other words, loudly.

 Theatre productions of the musical *Cats* used standard condoms to protect the body microphones worn by the cast.

The Grateful Dead

The lyrics of this rock group's rather esoteric song 'China Cat Sunflower' ends with the line *'In the eagle wing palace of the Queen Chinee'* — an adaptation of the same line in Dame Edith Sitwell's equally esoteric poem, 'Trio for Two Cats and a Trombone'.

Cat Stevens

He was born Steven Demetre Georgiou in Britain, to Greek-Cypriot and Swedish parents. He changed his name in his teenage years to become Cat Stevens, and enjoyed worldwide success as a singer/songwriter before converting from Greek Orthodox to Muslim. For that he changed his name again, to Yusuf Islam.

The Cat's Meow

In *Gypsy*, the musical version of strip star Gypsy Rose Lee's life (Sondheim, Laurent, Styne), the character of Tulsa is one of the dancing boys in the chorus. But he has ambition:

> Once my clothes were shabby,
> Tailors called me 'Cabbie',
> So I took a vow –
> Said this bum'll
> Be Beau Brummel.
> Now I'm smooth and snappy,
> Now my tailor's happy,
> I'm the cat's meow,
> My wardrobe is a wow!

9
Books and writers

Feline first

Thought to be the first serious book on cats, *Histoire des Chats* was written by François-Augustin de Paradis de Moncrif in 1727. Consisting mainly of letters praising particularly distinguished cats, de Moncrif tells about Marmalain (the beautiful cat of la Duchesse du Maine), Tata (the pet of la Marquise de Montglas), Dom Gris (who belonged to Duchesse Bethune), and the beautiful Menine (whose early death caused such grief to la Duchesse de Lesdiguières). We learn also of harpist Mlle du Puy's loving cat, who listened to her playing with critical attention — displaying pleasure if she played well, but annoyance if she made a mistake.

Alas, de Moncrif's work on cats was scorned by his contemporary literati to the extent that his reputation was endangered, and, when praise for his other writings caused him to be elected to the French Academy, he withdrew the cat book from circulation.

But while many of de Moncrif's esteemed contemporaries, and the noble works praised at the time — poems, pastorales, plays — are now almost totally obscure, de Moncrif's love of and writing about cats still keeps his name alive.

H. G. Wells

Wells is generally regarded as the world's first great writer of science fiction, and is not known to have any particular relationship with cats. But according to his famous novel *The Invisible Man* (1897), the project to make a man invisible could not have occurred without a cat. The character of his scientist, Griffin, admitted that he'd first tried out the drug on a cat, and succeeded — except for its eyes, because the back of a cat's eyes do not absorb light, they reflect it, which his 'invisibility' treatment could not overcome. So while the body of the cat could not be seen, the cat's eyes moved around the room in ghost-like fashion without the cat's body being visible around them.

Cats cannot actually see in total darkness. But the structure of a cat's eyes allows it to see quite clearly in only one-sixth of the light humans need to see clearly. In near-darkness, things barely visible to a human can be distinguished quite easily by a cat.

The back of cats' eyeballs includes a special reflective layer called the *tapetum lucidum*. This works like a mirror on the retina, reflecting light back through the eyes and giving the eyes a second chance to absorb the light. It helps cats see in very low light, and, because light is being reflected back out of them, the impression to the observer is that the eyes are glowing.

While H.G. Wells's scientist Griffin was of course fictional, his reasoning was correct, because his 'invisibility' relied on a body absorbing all light. However, the mirror-like *tapetum lucidum* did the opposite and reflected light back outwards … so the two eyes could be seen 'ghost-like' moving around the room.

 Shakespeare's works include 42 mentions of the cat. The Bible doesn't mention them. There you will find dogs, cattle, donkeys, lions, horses and chickens … but no cats.

Kit-Kat Club, London

Two such venues have had notable literary association. Eighteenth-century London bookseller Jacob Tonson began a series of gatherings in the premises of Christopher ('Kit') Catt, a maker of mutton pies. Known as the Kit-Kat Club, its 39 members included political and literary celebrities of the time. Mr Catt's premise had a low ceiling, and its walls could only accommodate paintings that were wider than they were high. For a time, paintings of this oblong shape were referred to as 'kit-kats' ... whose determinedly oblong shape is believed (several centuries later) to be the origin of the similarly shaped chocolate bar.

 Ernest Hemingway owned (at various times) 30 cats.

Kit-Kat Club, Berlin

Christopher Isherwood's collection of stories *Goodbye to Berlin* was published in 1939, introducing readers to another 'Kit-Kat Club' — a murky dive in 1930s Berlin, employing an untalented English singer of alternative lifestyle called Sally Bowles. The original book was turned into a play (*I Am a Camera*, 1951) then a musical (*Cabaret*, 1961) and eventually a film of the musical (1972). The film made extraordinary changes to large amounts of the original story, including changing the nationality of the leading character and making her a very fine singer ... but the Kit-Kat Club retained its seediness.

Panchatantra

This collection of animal fables was composed around AD 500 in the Sanskrit language, and is believed to have been created at the orders of an Indian rajah who wanted his three prince sons educated in manners and morals.

'The Lean Cat and the Fat Cat' tells of a humble old lady in a cottage whose pet cat was fed scraps and home-made broth. One day he met a plump and sleek puss, who persuaded him that a fine meal could be had by stealing morsels from the king's table. Defying the advice of the poor old woman, the lean cat sneaked into the palace — not knowing that the king had become fed up with cats stealing his meals and had that very day decreed that all cats that entered the dining hall would be killed. The fat cat had already heard this, and stayed away — but the lean cat padded in, and met his death.

The old woman wailed the moral of the story: 'Stay where you are safe, and the broth is honest. Steal and you court your doom.'

Training manual

Respected American animal trainer Miriam Fields-Babineau is author of over 40 books, mainly about the care, breeds and training of dogs. Apart from her dog titles, one of her books suggests impressive optimism: *Cat Training in 10 Minutes*. Ms Fields-Babineau is confident that by following the instructions she outlines (with many featured photos), you can train your pet to respond to your wish that Puss will sit, jump, retrieve, stay, and walk on a lead — and adjust to other desired conformities.

Boswell writing about Dr Samuel Johnson

I never shall forget the indulgence with which he
treated Hodge, his cat: for whom he himself used to
go out and buy oysters, lest the servants having that
trouble should take a dislike to the poor creature
... I recollect [Hodge] one day scrambling up Dr
Johnson's breast, apparently with much satisfaction,
while my friend smiling and half-whistling, rubbed
down his back, and pulled him by the tail; and
when I observed he was a fine cat, saying 'Why yes,
Sir, but I have had cats whom I liked better than
this' and then as if perceiving Hodge to be out of
countenance, adding, 'but he is a very fine cat, a
very fine cat indeed.'

— Boswell, *Life of Johnson*

Hodge's statue

In Gough Square, London, Dr Samuel Johnson's cat Hodge,
who died c.1784, has his own life-size bronze memorial
statue. It was unveiled in September 1997, by the Lord
Mayor of London, Sir Roger Cook, and shows Hodge sitting
on a dictionary. Percival Stockdale wrote 'An Elegy on the
Death of Dr Johnson's Favourite Cat', from which we learn
that Hodge was a black cat:

Who, by his master when caressed
Warmly his gratitude expressed;
And never failed his thanks to purr
Whene'er he stroked his sable fur.

Journal of a Voyage to Lisbon, 1754

A most tragical incident fell out this day at sea. While the ship was under sail, but making as will appear no great way, a kitten, one of four of the feline inhabitants of the cabin, fell from the window into the water: an alarm was immediately given to the captain, who was then upon deck, and received it with the utmost concern and many bitter oaths. He immediately gave orders to the steersman in favour of the poor thing, as he called it; the sails were instantly slackened, and all hands, as the phrase is, employed to recover the poor animal. I was, I own, extremely surprised at all this; less indeed at the captain's extreme tenderness than at his conceiving any possibility of success; for if puss had had nine thousand instead of nine lives, I concluded they had been all lost. The boatswain, however, had more sanguine hopes, for, having stripped himself of his jacket, breeches, and shirt, he leaped boldly into the water, and to my great astonishment in a few minutes returned to the ship, bearing the motionless animal in his mouth. Nor was this, I observed, a matter of such great difficulty as it appeared to my ignorance, and possibly may seem to that of my fresh-water reader. The kitten was now exposed to air and sun on the deck, where its life, of which it retained no symptoms, was despaired of by all.

The captain's humanity, if I may so call it, did not so totally destroy his philosophy as to make him yield himself up to affliction on this melancholy occasion. Having felt his loss like a man, he resolved to show he could bear it like one; and, having declared he had rather have lost a cask of rum or brandy, betook himself to threshing at backgammon with the Portuguese friar, in which innocent amusement they had passed about two-thirds of their time.

But as I have, perhaps, a little too wantonly endeavoured to raise the tender passions of my readers in this narrative, I should think myself unpardonable if I concluded it without giving them the satisfaction of hearing that the kitten at last recovered, to the great joy of the good captain, but to the great disappointment of some of the sailors, who asserted that the drowning of a cat was the very surest way of raising a favorable wind; a supposition of which, though we have heard several plausible accounts, we will not presume to assign the true original reason.

— Henry Fielding (d.1754)

Catmopolitan

In 1987, the magazine *Cosmopolitan* published a one-off mirror image of itself — but entirely concerned with cats. All the advertising consisted of 'cat' versions of standard products, and text articles included witty features on fashions and feline style, beauty tips, food and diet advice, and even letters asking for personal guidance in intimate matters. *Catmopolitan* had been inspired by the earlier *Dogue*, the canine version of a well-known fashion magazine.

The Silent Miaow

The Silent Miaow is a book written by a cat, and 'translated from the feline' by Paul Gallico. It has advice on property rights, food, behaviour and protocol.

Ulysses

In James Joyce's *Ulysses*, a cat's noise is described as 'cat's ululation', which started as (Joyce's invented word) *'mkgano'*. But as the cat became more demanding (of milk) its sound becomes louder and is depicted as *'mrkgano'*.

Reflexology

Reflexology: a therapy involving pressure applied to specific differing places on the sole of the foot — creating a reflex which influences corresponding parts of, and functions of, the body's anatomy.

Jackie Segers, a Reiki master and graduate of the American Academy of Reflexology, Encino, became interested in improving the quality of life for her pets, by introducing reflexology into their routines. Her 2007 book, *Reflexology for Cats*, gives careful and detailed guidance for treating your pet with thumb pressure on identified regions of the upturned paws.

The book's diagrammatic cat 'paw maps' identify and divide the paw and its pads into areas which correspond to the cat's body parts and systems. Ms Segers explains that thumb massage on designated paw places will help: soothe cat arthritis; aid constipation or diarrhoea; relieve a cat's stress, asthma or kidney failure; balance its emotional moods; and complement treatment for diabetes.

Ms Segers includes advice on ear reflexology — aka 'auriclotherapy' — stimulating the cat's outer ear to assist in healing the mind, body and spirit of the cat. An 'ear map' shows which pressure points on the cat's ear connect to its chest, spine, jaw or pelvic regions.

(A related book is the tongue-in-cheek *Pawmistry* by Ken Ring, detailing how a cat's character traits can be observed in its paws ...)

Cat Among the Pigeons

Agatha Christie's 1959 novel *Cat Among the Pigeons* is not about actual cats: the story is centred around a heady mix containing jewels, an exotic prince, nervous schoolgirls — and Hercules Poirot.

 Charles Dickens's white cat William surprised him one day by producing kittens. Dickens re-named the cat Williamina.

Lilith

The shadowy figure of Lilith — supposed first wife of Adam — was banished from Eden and became forever after associated with images of evil. One version of her story has her becoming a monster vampire who liked to disguise herself as a large black cat. Other depictions of her show a woman's face on a cat's body.

Astrology

It might not be only humans whose lives are subject to astrological influences and the effects of their zodiac birth signs. At least four different authors have studied and published the interpretations of the significance of the zodiac on cats. We are told that knowing the birth-date of a cat will explain their temperament, behaviour patterns, and potential relationships with other animals — including humans. Choose from:

- *Cat Astrology* (Mary Daniels)

- *The Cat Horoscope Book* (Liz Tresilian)

- *Catsigns: Lunar Astrological Guide to Cats* (William Fairchild)

- *Your Cat's Lifetime Horoscope* (Luba Matusovsky)

- *The Complete Book of Feline Horoscopes* (Michael Zullo)

- *The Cat Horoscope Book* (Henry Cole)

- *Horoscopes for Each of Your Cat's Nine Lives* (Genia Wennerstrom)

Very helpfully, some authors suggest which zodiac sign of the owner would mesh best with which zodiac sign of a potential pet cat ...

Thomas Carlyle's cat was named Columbine.

Lewis Carroll

In a letter to a friend's child, author Lewis Carroll wrote a whimsical (and fictional) account of when three stray cats had come to his door. He reported that he took them in and they slept the night between sheets of blotting paper. Then for breakfast he cooked them 'rat-tail jelly and buttered mice'.

Buddhist cat

Many books tell of cat-owners' love for, and adventures with, their own cats. Some are even written 'by' the cat. Among the latter, David Michie, author of several successful books on Buddhism, presents an endearing albeit imaginary 'biography' written from the point of view of a rather special creature: *The Dalai Lama's Cat*. The street stray, born in New Delhi (with a complete command of English), becomes the loved pet of the Dalai Lama, and an adherent of the master's philosophy and teachings. But although observing the Buddhist belief in non-violence, the puss does not entirely lose any cat characteristics, and at one point memorably proclaims:

We cats are not robotic beasts who can be conditioned to sit down or salivate at the utterance of a command or the press of a bell. Did you ever hear of a Pavlov cat?

(Good point. We also do not hear of 'police' cats, 'airport' cats, 'guide' cats, etc.)

Mehitabel

This colourful cat character was created by Don Marquis. Mehitabel is convinced that in her former life she had been Cleopatra. Her current incarnation is rather less grand than Cleopatra and a bit threadbare (but *'toujours gai'*), and she is a friend of Archie the cockroach. When the adventures of the cockroach and the cat became the Broadway musical *Shinbone Alley* in 1957, Mehitabel was played by Eartha Kitt.

Foss

Edward Lear's cat Foss was partly the source of some of the cats in his nonsense poems, such as 'The Owl and the Pussy-Cat'. (See **The Owl and the Pussy-Cat**.)

Webster

P. G. Wodehouse's tale 'The Story of Webster' tells of the unfortunate Lancelot Mulliner, who is obliged to look after his rich uncle's cat for a period. Uncle Theodore has strict standards which he claims are shared by the cat.

> **'Webster is an example of upright conduct which cannot but act as an antidote to the poison cup of temptation which is no doubt hourly pressed to your lips.'**

And indeed, dominated by the presence of the superior cat, Lancelot's lifestyle becomes depressingly restricted … until the day cat Webster samples some spilt rum, and likes it so much he becomes totally blotto. Subsequently, a more relaxed mood grows between Lancelot and Webster the cat.

Tobermory

Unlike the rest of the cats in the world, who communicate through vocalising and varied body language, Tobermory has the unusual ability to speak English. This he does at a high-class weekend party, to the amazement of the guests in Saki's *Chronicles of Clovis* (1911). Here is a sample of Tobermory's style:

'What do you think of human intelligence?' asked Mavis Pellington lamely.

'Of whose intelligence in particular?' asked Tobermory coldly.

'Oh, well, mine for instance,' said Mavis with a feeble laugh.

'You put me in an embarrassing position,' said Tobermory, whose tone and attitude certainly did not suggest a shred of embarrassment.

'When your inclusion in this house-party was suggested Sir Wilfrid protested that you were the most brainless woman of his acquaintance, and that there was a wide distinction between hospitality and the care of the feeble-minded. Lady Blemley replied that your lack of brain-power was the precise quality which had earned you your invitation, as you were the only person she could think of who might be idiotic enough to buy their old car. You know, the one they call "The Envy of Sisyphus," because it goes quite nicely up-hill if you push it.'

Major Barfield plunged in heavily to effect a diversion.

'How about your carryings-on with the tortoise-shell puss up at the stables, eh?'

The moment he had said it every one realized the blunder.

'One does not usually discuss these matters in public,' said Tobermory frigidly. 'From a slight observation of your ways since you've been in this house I should imagine you'd find it inconvenient if I were to shift the conversation to your own little affairs ...'

Cats paint and dance?

New Zealand author Burton Silver and illustrator Heather Busch produced an amusing book of inspired silliness called *Why Cats Paint*. Described as 'An unprecedented photographic record of cat creativity that will intrigue cat-lovers and art lovers alike', it became an international bestseller, initiating much discussion about whether the cats actually were painting on canvases ... or was it photo-adjustment?

Undeterred, Silver and Busch moved on to an (equally successful) sequel: *Dancing with Cats* — about people dancing with cats, and cats dancing with people. Sold as 'Some people whisper to horses; others dance with cats. Both are manifestations of humankind's continual striving to connect with their animal companions on a higher spiritual level.'

Any doubt about the sincerity or truthfulness of the author's claims (and photographs) was obscured by the charm and wackiness of the ideas — and the immaculate way they were presented.

Mary Shelley

Mary Shelley, author of *Frankenstein*, had other less gruesome mystic beliefs. She once told her brother (poet Percy Shelley), 'Come and look — here's a cat eating roses, she'll turn into a woman! When beasts eat these roses they turn into men and women!' (With all due respect to Mary Shelley, there is no record of its being seen happening.)

Swyft, plyante and mery ...

The catte is a beaste of uncertain heare and colour, for some catte is white, some rede, some black, some skewed and speckled in the fete and in the face and in the eares.

And he is in youth swyfte, plyante and mery and lepeth and reseth on all thynge that is tofore him; and is led by a strawe and playeth therewith. And is a right hevy beast in age, and ful slepy, and lieth slily in wait for myce. And he maketh a ruthfull noyse and gustful when one proffereth to fythte with another.

— Bartholomew Glanvil, *De Rerum Natura* (1398)

Bertie Wooster's Augustus

Wodehouse's character Bertie Wooster once explained (in *Jeeves in the Offing*) that a cat called Augustus suffers from permanent lethargy. To substantiate his observation, Bertie explains to a housemaid that this particular lethargy is scientifically named 'traumatic symplegia', described as:

> where other cats are content to get their eight hours, Augustus wants his twenty-four.

Alas, Bertie's erudition may have impressed the housemaid, but bears the stamp of improvisation: traumatic symplegia is unknown to the *OED*.

Library cats

In the United States, the Library Cat Society was founded in 1987, encouraging libraries to have cats in attendance.

'Wonderland' cat

Lewis Carroll's *Alice's Adventures in Wonderland* features a young English girl whose pet cat is Dinah — although Dinah never actually appears in the story.

Cheshire

Carroll's famous Cheshire cat explains to Alice that a dog growls when he is angry and wags his tail when he is happy, but a cat growls when he is happy and wags his tail when he is angry. Alice doesn't agree that a cat 'growls': 'I call it purring, not growling,' she says.

Victor Hugo, author of *Les Misérables,* called his pet cat Mouche — French for 'fly'.

'Walks by himself'

Rudyard Kipling, in 'The Cat that Walked by Himself', asserts that mankind has domesticated dogs, cows and horses. But the cat:

> will kill mice and he will be kind to Babies when he is in the house, just as long as they do not pull his tail too hard. But when he has done that, and between times, and when the moon gets up and night comes, he is the Cat that walks by himself, and all places are alike to him …

Mrs T. Twitchit

Beatrix Potter's stories include the charming cat Mrs Tabitha Twitchit and her family: Tom Kitten, Moppett and Mittens.

Aesop

In 500 BC Aesop used animals to make moral points. Some of his tales concern cats involved with an eagle, Venus, a fox, a young mouse, and a cockerel.

 Lord Byron's cat Beppo travelled everywhere with him.

The Cat in the Hat

An article in *Life* in May 1954 examined a perceived falling in the literacy rate of American schoolchildren, perhaps because their assigned books were boring. Writer Theodore Geisel met the challenge. Together with his publisher, Geisel compiled a list of 250 words considered 'important' to help children learn reading, and then Geisel set to work to make a story out of those words and to illustrate it.

Using the pen-name 'Dr Seuss', in 1957 he wrote *The Cat in the Hat* — using only 223 words. *The Cat in the Hat* became legendary, and was translated into 27 languages. Ever since, the book has been in the Top 10 bestselling hardcover books for children. It was the forerunner of 43 other children's books by Dr Seuss, with sales of over 200 million copies.

Thomas Gray

'All that glitters is not gold' is a mis-quote from Thomas Gray's poem 'Ode on the Death of a Favourite Cat, Drowned in a Tub of Gold Fishes', where the luckless cat is reminded that:

> **Not all that tempts your wandering eyes**
> **And heedless hearts, is lawful prize;**
> **Nor all that glisters gold.**

Poe's black cat

Edgar Allan Poe's horrifying short story 'The Black Cat' (1843) dispels any belief which pragmatists might hold that cats cannot possibly have mystic powers.

Garfield

Besides the other books 'written' by Garfield (including advice on how to accept the admiration of others, and how to whip a flabby ego into shape), in 1988 he published *The Garfield Book of Cat Names*, an intriguing collection of over 250 suggested names to accord with a cat's type, gender and habits. He included some which earn his scorn: for example, Muffin, Kitty and Snowball are dismissed as inane names no self-respecting cats would allow.

Puss in Boots

This familiar figure has appeared in European legends for centuries – he can be found in Italian folk tales of 1554. A century later the famous collection of fables and legends collected and re-told by French writer Charles Perrault in 1697, was published as *Tales from Mother Goose*. Included was the Puss in Boots story familiar to English speaking children ever since: the clever cat who helps his master secure a fortune — and a beautiful bride.

Mark Twain

During most of his busy year, American author Mark Twain felt unable to properly care for cats, but he liked them around the home during his summer holiday. So from a local farmer he 'rented' cats to share the summer months with him. One was black, the other grey ... he called one Sackcloth and the other one Ashes.

At other times Mark Twain owned cats named Blatherskite, Zoroaster, Sin, Satan, Tammany, Apollinaris and Sour Mash.

10
Poetry

'Pangur Bán'

One of the earliest known cats with a name emerges in European literature, from between the eighth and ninth centuries. An Irish Benedictine monk living in a monastery where Germany meets Austria wrote of his cat Pangur Bán, who, as the author sitting alone in his study was seeking the significance of words, was seeking mice.

The ancient four-page manuscript was discovered nearly a thousand years after it was written, and was published in 1903.

The monk muses over eight stanzas, observing his cat Pangur Bán and the amiable relationship between them – in spite of their apparently differing lifestyles.

> I and Pángur Ban my cat,
> 'Tis a like task we are at:
> Hunting mice is his delight,
> Hunting words I sit all night.

Shakespeare uses the phrase 'Ding, dong, bell' in *The Merchant of Venice*, Act III:

> Let us all ring fancy's knell;
> I'll begin it — Ding, dong, bell.

And in *The Tempest*, Act I, Scene II:

> Sea nymphs hourly ring his knell: Ding dong.
> Hark! now I hear them — Ding, dong, bell.

The cat in the well

Ding, dong, bell, pussy's in the well.
Who put her in? Little Tommy Thin.
Who pulled her out? Little Tommy Stout.
What a naughty boy was that,
To drown poor Pussy Cat,
Who never did him any harm,
But killed the mice in his father's barn!

Versions of this very old rhyme date back to the late sixteenth century. The song is sometimes seen as representing the feudal waifs and wretches who were born to serve their noble lords without question and died without any appreciation from those they had served.

Others see it more simply: just encouraging children to understand that when an animal has done no harm it is unfair to treat it cruelly.

During the nineteenth century, scholastic amusement some-times translated familiar nursery rhymes into Latin. Such as:

Hei! didulim! atque iterum didulim! Felisque fidesque
Vacca super lunae cornua prosiluit;
Nescio qua catulus risit dulcedine ludi;
Abstulit et turpi lanx cochleare fuga.

For which read:

Hey diddle diddle, the cat and the fiddle
The cow jumped over the moon, etc.

The cat and the fiddle

Hey diddle diddle, the cat and the fiddle,
The cow jumped over the moon.
The little dog laughed to see such fun
And the dish ran away with the spoon!

First published in 1765 (as 'High Diddle Diddle') any explanation of exactly what this song meant has been lost in the mists of time. One theory is that it may be the nonsense result of juxtaposing the goods kept in a poor home: a cat to keep mice under control; a dog to protect the family; a cow for milk; a dish and spoon for the table; and a fiddle for singing and dancing.

Two fanciful references to the familiar ditty appear in J. R. R. Tolkien's *The Adventures of Tombadil*, sung by Frodo, and in *The Hobbit: An Unexpected Journey*, sung by Bofur.

Old Possum's Book of Practical Cats

T. S. Eliot wrote this collection of amusing poems in 1939, and it went on sale for 3/6d (35 cents). Forty-two years later, Andrew Lloyd Webber turned the poems into the musical *Cats* which opened in May 1981. The musical was translated into 10 languages, and was performed in 300 cities across 26 countries. Within 10 years, *Cats* had done $US1 billion worth of business.

It is somehow hard to imagine that happening with a musical called *Dogs*.

'The Owl and the Pussy-Cat'

The Owl and the Pussy-Cat went to sea
In a beautiful pea-green boat.
They took some honey, and plenty of money,
Wrapped up in a five-pound note.
The Owl looked up to the stars above,
And sang to a small guitar,
'O lovely Pussy! O Pussy, my love,
What a beautiful Pussy you are,
You are,
You are!
What a beautiful Pussy you are!'

Pussy said to the Owl, 'You elegant fowl!
How charmingly sweet you sing!
O let us be married! too long we have tarried:
But what shall we do for a ring?'
They sailed away, for a year and a day,
To the land where the Bong-Tree grows,
And there in a wood a Piggy-wig stood,
With a ring at the end of his nose,
His nose,
His nose,
With a ring at the end of his nose.

'Dear Pig, are you willing to sell for one shilling
Your ring?' Said the Piggy, 'I will.'
So they took it away, and were married next day
By the Turkey who lives on the hill.
They dined on mince, and slices of quince,
Which they ate with a runcible spoon;
And hand in hand on the edge of the sand
They danced by the light of the moon,
The moon,
The moon,
They danced by the light of the moon.

Edward Lear d.1888

A totally whimsical and endearing 'nonsense poem' said to have been inspired by Lear's own cat. Part of the poem's charm is its totally ridiculous juxtaposition of images (mince and slices of quince are hardly everyday fare) and the mystery which still surrounds exactly what a 'runcible' spoon is. Someone proposed that it was one of those broad three-pronged forks commonly used for pickles, but it was only *proposed* — nobody actually knows. There is a possibility the poet was echoing the old word *rouncival* which meant large, even gigantic. But more than possible is that, like the Bong-Tree, Lear simply invented it.

The cat and the Queen

Pussy-cat, Pussy-cat where have you been?
I've been to London to look at the Queen.
Pussy-cat, Pussy-cat, what did you there?
I frightened a little mouse under a chair.

It is usually believed that the Queen in question was
Elizabeth I, whose retinue was known to include one courtier
with an old cat which plodded around palaces indiscrimin-
ately, and once ventured underneath the Queen's throne
when she was sitting on it. Elizabeth was startled, then
amused, and announced that the cat had the freedom of the
throne room, providing it kept the area free of mice.

'This is the House that Jack Built'

The poem 'This is the House that Jack Built' may date as far
back as the thirteenth century, and its 'cumulative' structure
may be based on the ancient Hebrew chant about the kid-goat
bought for two farthings. By 1750, when it first appeared in
print, 'The House that Jack Built' may have been referring to
the mythical character John Bull. But, whatever its mysteries,
the poem certainly features:

This is the cat
That killed the rat
That ate the malt
That lay in the house that Jack built.

174

St Ives

As I was going to St Ives,
I met a man with seven wives;
Every wife had seven sacks;
Every sack had seven cats;
Every cat had seven kits.
Kits, cats, sacks and wives,
How many were there going to St Ives?

Apart from the unlikelihood of a man having seven wives all at one time, the verse is a riddle as well as a nursery rhyme — a nonsense song intended to exercise a child's logic rather than their arithmetic skills.

How many were going to St Ives?
Why, only one person of course. Think about it ... the others were all *coming away* from St Ives.

'The Owl and the Panther'

I passed by his garden, and marked
 with one eye,
How the Owl and the Panther were
 sharing a pie:
The Panther took pie-crust, and gravy,
 and meat,
While the Owl had the dish as its share
 of the treat.
When the pie was all finished, the Owl,
 as a boon,
Was kindly permitted to pocket the
 spoon:
While the Panther received knife and
 fork with a growl
And concluded the banquet by . . .

Lewis Carroll, d.1898

Lewis Carroll's nonsense poem deliberately leaves out the last three words ('eating the owl'), encouraging the listening children to relish the *Schadenfreude* of filling in the words themselves.

11
Smile and reflect

The Cat of Cats

I am the cat of cats. I am
The everlasting cat.
Cunning, and old, and sleek as jam,
The everlasting cat.
I hunt the vermin in the night
The everlasting cat,
For I see best without the light —
The everlasting cat.

William Brighty Rands (1823–82)

The cat was created from the sneeze of a lion.

Arabian proverb

There are two means of refuge from the miseries of life
— music and cats.

Albert Schweitzer

Cats, flies and women are ever at their toilets.

French proverb

If your cat falls out of a tree, go indoors to laugh.

Patricia Hitchcock

To carry a cat across water in your arms
will bring bad luck.

French superstition

Cats like doors to be left open – in case
they change their minds.

Rosemary Nisbet

There was an old bulldog named Caesar
Who went for a cat, just to tease her
But she spat and she spit
Till the poor bulldog quit
Now when poor Caesar sees her,
   he flees her.

 If a cat swallows a coin – there is
money in the kitty!

Anon

Cats are intended to teach us that not everything
in nature has a purpose.

Garrison Keillor

 If a cat washes behind its ears, there will be rain.

British folklore

Dogs come when they're called, cats take a message
and get back to you later.

Mary Bly

A dog will often steal a bone
But conscience lets him not alone,
And by his tail his guilt is known.

But cats consider theft as game
And, howsoever you may blame,
Refuse the slightest sign of shame.

Anon

 Cats are God's way of telling you
your furniture is too nice.

There is no need of sculpture in a home which has a cat.

Wesley Bates

 Humans – no fur, no tail, they run
away from mice, they never get
enough sleep. How can a cat help
but love such an absurd animal?

To a Cat

Stately, kindly, lordly friend
Condescend
Here to sit by me, and turn
Glorious eyes that smile and burn,
Golden eyes, love's lustrous meed*
On the golden page I read.

All your wondrous wealth of hair,
Dark and fair,
Silken-shaggy, soft and bright
As the clouds and beams of night,
Pays my reverent hand's caress
Back with friendlier gentleness.

Dogs may fawn on all and some
As they come;
You, a friend of loftier mind,
Answer friends alone in kind.
Just your foot upon my hand
Softly bids it understand.

Algernon Charles Swinburne (1837 1909)

* meed — old word for *reward*.

Fair-haired little girls, books and cats
make the best furniture for a room.

French proverb

The clever cat eats cheese and breathes down
rat holes with baited breath.

W.C. Fields

 Rats don't dance in the cat's doorway.
(Meaning: don't push your luck)

African proverb

In order to keep a true perspective of one's importance,
everyone should have a dog that will worship him
and a cat that will ignore him.

Dereke Bruce

 Was it a car or a cat I saw?
(Palindrome)

My cat does not talk as respectfully to me as I do to her.

Colette

Cat mantra: 'Sleep and eat,
eat and sleep, sleep and
eat – is there no end
to this overwork?

Who could believe such pleasure from
a wee ball o' fur?

Irish saying

Dogs have owners – cats have staff.

Rita Mae Brown

Kittens, you are very little,
And your kitten bones are brittle,
If you'd grow to cats respected,
See your play be not neglected.

Smite the Sudden Spool, and spring
Upon the Swift Elusive String,
Thus you learn to catch the wary
Mister Mouse or Miss Canary.

Oliver Herford (1863–1935)

The man who doesn't love cats will never
have a pretty woman.

Dutch proverb

One is never sure, watching two cats washing each other,
whether it's affection, the taste, or a trial run for the jugular.

Helen Thomson

She Sights a Bird

She sights a bird — she chuckles —
She flattens — then she crawls —
She runs without the look of feet
Her eyes increase to balls —

Her jaws stir — twitching — hungry —
Her teeth can hardly stand —
She leaps, but Robin leaped the first —
Ah, Pussy of the sand,

The hopes so juicy ripening —
You almost bathed your tongue —
When Bliss disclosed a hundred toes —
And fled with every one.

Emily Dickinson (1830–86)

Cats are smarter than dogs. You'd never get eight cats
to pull a sled through the snow.

Jeff Valdez

If cats had wings, there would be no ducks
left in the lake.

Indian saying

When a cat has eaten a whole duck ...
it is a duck-filled-fatty-puss.

Dogs eat. Cats dine.

Ann Taylor

 Macrobiotic cats eat only brown mice.

A cat's worst enemy is a closed door.

A rose has thorns, a cat has
claws. Both are worth the risk.

 Purranoia: A condition found in humans who
fear that the cat is up to something.

To err is human, to purr is feline.

Robert Byrne

If cats could talk, they wouldn't.

Nan Porter

 It is better to feed one cat than many mice.

Norwegian proverb

A cat in distress,
Nothing more, nor less;
Good folks, I must faithfully tell ye,
As I am a sinner,
It wants for some dinner
To stuff out its own little belly.

You mightn't easily guess
All the modes of distress
Which torture the tenants of earth;
And the various evils,
Which like many devils,
Attend the poor dogs from their birth.

Some a living require,
And others desire
An old fellow out of the way;
And which is the best
I leave to be guessed,
For I cannot pretend to say.

One wants society,
Another variety,
Others a tranquil life;
Some want food,
Others, as good,
Only require a wife.

But this poor little cat
Only wanted a rat,
To stuff out its own little maw;
And it were as good
Had some people such food,
To make them hold their jaw.

Percy Bysshe Shelley (1792–1822). It is believed that he wrote
this poem in 1802, when he was ten years old.

 A cat sneezing is a good omen for
everyone who hears it.

Italian folklore

I had been told that the training procedure with cats was difficult.
It's not. Mine had me trained in two days.

Bill Dana

 A cat knows your every thought.
Knows, but doesn't care.

Anon

The moving cat sheds, and
having shed, moves on …

My husband said it was him or the cat.
I miss him sometimes.

Anon

Last Words to a Dumb Friend

Housemate I can think you still
Bounding to the window sill,
Over which I vaguely see
Your small mound beneath a tree
Showing in the Autumn shade
That you moulder where you played.

Thomas Hardy (1840–1928)

If at Christmas you have a dream wherein
a black cat appears, then within the following
year you will have an illness.

German folklore

The Cat and the Pudding String

Sing, sing, what shall I sing?
The cat's run away with the pudding string!
Do, do, what shall I do?
The cat has bitten it quite in two.

Sing, sing, what shall I sing?
The cat has eaten the pudding string!
Do, do, what shall I do?
The cat's run away with the pudding too.

Anon

Whether they be real cats or the musician cats
in my band – they all got style!

Ray Charles

 Mohammed stroked his cat three times down
its spine – thus giving it the power always
to land on its feet.

Muslim folklore

Cruel, but composed and bland,
Dumb, inscrutable and grand,
So Tiberius might have sat,
Had Tiberius been a cat.

Matthew Arnold (1822–88)

Two Little Kittens

Two little kittens, one stormy night,
Began to quarrel, and then to fight;
One had a mouse, the other had none,
And that's the way the quarrel begun.

'I'll have that mouse,' said the biggest cat;
'You'll have that mouse? We'll see about that!'
'I *will* have that mouse,' said the eldest son;
'You *shan't* have the mouse,' said the little one.

I told you before 'twas a stormy night
When these two little kittens began to fight;
The old woman seized her sweeping broom,
And swept the two kittens right out of the room.

The ground was all covered with frost and snow,
And the two little kittens had nowhere to go;
So they laid them down on the mat at the door,
While the old woman finished sweeping the floor.

Then they crept in, as quiet as mice,
All wet with snow, and cold as ice,
For they found it was better, that stormy night,
To lie down and sleep than to quarrel and fight.

Anon, *c.* 1879

When moving into a new home, put the cat
through the window instead of the door
… then it will not leave.

American folklore

Kittens are born with their eyes shut … They open them
in about six days, take a look around, then close them
again for the better part of their lives.

Stephen Baker

Said a miserly lord at the Abbey,
'I fear I shall look rather shabby,
For I've replaced my ermine,
Infested with vermin,
With the fur of my dear defunct tabby.'

Anon

When the world began, the sun created the lion
and the moon created the cat.

Ancient Greek belief

Thou art the Great Cat, the avenger of the
Gods, and the judge of words, and the
president of the sovereign chiefs and the
governor of the holy circle.

Inscription on the Royal Tombs at Thebes in Egypt

MEOW
A book of happiness for cat lovers

Meow is a compendium of fine quotes that capture the essence of our fascination with cats, accompanied by a selection of superb photographs showing our feline friends in all their moods. This beautiful book makes an ideal gift.

FELINE FRIENDS
Tales from the heart

The Cat Protection Society of NSW Inc.

The stories in this engaging book range from the hilarious to the poignant and show why we find cats so captivating and endearing. They include cats who 'adopted' their owners, malnourished strays who dropped in just long enough to entrust the householder with their kittens, loving companions brightening the old age of their devoted owners, and little bundles of fur given as a child's first pet. The accompanying photographs have never been published before.

FOR THE LOVE OF A CAT
A publisher's story

David St John Thomas

Vividly written, sometimes serious, sometimes light-hearted, this uplifting story is one man's homage to the cats in his life. A spirited cast of feline characters step off these pages, or perhaps lie curled in seductive curves upon them.